The SINKING of the TITANIC

THRILLING STORIES OF SURVIVORS
WITH PHOTOGRAPHS & SKETCHES

NIMBUS
PUBLISHING

Nimbus Publishing, 1998
First published in 1912, L. T. Myers

Nimbus Publishing Limited
PO Box 9301, Station A
Halifax, NS   B3K 5N5
(902) 455-4286

Printed and bound by Printcrafters Inc.

ISBN 1-55109-251-4

Canadian Cataloguing in Publication Data

Main entry under title:
The sinking of the Titanic
Originally published as: The sinking of the Titanic and great sea disasters. Philadelphia: C. Winston, 1912.
ISBN 1-55109-251-4
1. Titanic (Steamship) 2. Shipwrecks-North Atlantic Ocean.
I. Marshall, Logan.
G530.T6S56 1998   910'.9163'4   C98-950123-X

Publisher's note:
Because the original edition of this book was published in 1912 before all of the information concerning the disaster had been verified, some inaccuracies appear in the text.

THE TITANIC

The largest and finest steamship in the world; on her maiden voyage, loaded with a human freight of over 2,300 souls, she collided with a huge iceberg 600 miles southeast of Halifax, at 11.40 P. M., Sunday, April 14, 1912, and sank two and a half hours later, carrying over 1,600 of her passengers and crew with her.

CAPTAIN E. J. SMITH
Of the ill-fated giant of the sea; a brave and seasoned commander who was carried to his death with his last and greatest ship.

Dedication

To the 1635 souls who were lost with the ill-fated Titanic, and especially to those heroic men, who, instead of trying to save themselves, stood aside that women and children might have their chance; of each of them let it be written, as it was written of a Greater One—

"He Died that Others might Live"

CONTENTS

FACTS ABOUT THE WRECK OF THE TITANIC

N UMBER of persons aboard, 2340.
Number of life-boats and rafts, 20.
Capacity of each life-boat, 50 passengers and crew of 8.
Utmost capacity of life-boats and rafts, about 1100.
Number of life-boats wrecked in launching, 4.
Capacity of life-boats safely launched, 928.
Total number of persons taken in life-boats, 711.
Number who died in life-boats, 60
Total number saved, 705.
Total number of Titanic's company lost, 1635.

The cause of the disaster was a collision with an iceberg in latitude 41.46 north, longitude 50.14 west. The Titanic had had repeated warnings of the presence of ice in that part of the course. Two official warnings had been received defining the position of the ice fields. It had been calculated on the Titanic that she would reach the ice fields about 11 o'clock Sunday night. The collision occurred at 11.40. At that time the ship was driving at a speed of 21 to 23 knots, or about 26 miles an hour.

There had been no details of seamen assigned to each boat.

Some of the boats left the ship without seamen enough to man the oars. Some of the boats were not more than half full of passengers. The boats had no provisions. Some of them had no water stored, some were without sail equipment or compasses. In some boats, which carried sails wrapped and bound, there was not a person with a knife to cut the ropes. In some boats the plugs in the bottom had been pulled out and the women passengers were compelled to thrust their hands into the holes to keep the boats from filling and sinking. The captain, E. J. Smith, admiral of the White Star fleet, went down with his ship.

CHAPTER I

"THE TITANIC IN COLLISION, BUT EVERYBODY SAFE"—ANOTHER TRIUMPH SET DOWN TO WIRELESS TELEGRAPHY—THE WORLD GOES TO SLEEP PEACEFULLY—THE SAD AWAKENING.

L IKE a bolt out of a clear sky came the wireless message on Monday, April 15, 1912, that on Sunday night the great Titanic, on her maiden voyage across the Atlantic, had struck a gigantic iceberg, but that all the passengers were saved. The ship had signaled her distress and another victory was set down to wireless. Twenty-one hundred lives saved!

Additional news was soon received that the ship had collided with a mountain of ice in the North Atlantic, off Cape Race, Newfoundland, at 10.25 Sunday evening, April 14th. At 4.15 Monday morning the Canadian Government Marine Agency received a wireless message that the Titanic was sinking and that the steamers towing her were trying to get her into shoal water near Cape Race, for the purpose of beaching her.

Wireless despatches up to noon Monday showed that the passengers of the Titanic were being transferred aboard the steamer Carpathia, a Cunarder, which left New York, April 13th, for Naples. Twenty boatloads of the Titanic's passengers were said to have been transferred to the Carpathia then, and allowing forty to sixty persons as the capacity of each life-boat, some 800 or 1200 persons had already been transferred from the damaged liner to the Carpathia. They were reported as being taken to Halifax, whence they would be sent by train to New York.

Another liner, the Parisian, of the Allan Company, which sailed from Glasgow for Halifax on April 6th, was said to be close at hand and assisting in the work of rescue. The Baltic, Virginian and Olympic were also near the scene, according to the information received by wireless.

While badly damaged, the giant vessel was reported as still afloat, but whether she could reach port or shoal water was uncertain. The White Star officials declared that the Titanic was in no immediate danger of sinking, because of her numerous water-tight compartments.

"While we are still lacking definite information," Mr. Franklin, vice-president of the White Star Line, said later in the afternoon, "we believe the Titanic's passengers will reach Halifax, Wednesday evening. We have received no further word from Captain Haddock, of the Olympic, or from any of the ships in the vicinity, but are confident that there will be no loss of life."

With the understanding that the survivors would be taken to Halifax the line arranged to have thirty Pullman cars, two diners and many passenger coaches leave Boston Monday night for Halifax to get the passengers after they were landed.

Mr. Franklin made a guess that the Titanic's passengers would get into Halifax on Wednesday. The Department of Commerce and Labor notified the White Star Line that customs and immigration inspectors would be sent from Montreal to Halifax in order that there would be as little delay as possible in getting the passengers on trains.

Monday night the world slept in peace and assurance. A wireless message had finally been received, reading:

"All Titanic's passengers safe."

It was not until nearly a week later that the fact was discovered that this message had been wrongly received in the confusion of messages flashing through the air, and that in reality the message should have read:

"Are all Titanic's passengers safe?"

With the dawning of Tuesday morning came the awful news of the true fate of the Titanic.

CHAPTER II

THE MOST SUMPTUOUS PALACE AFLOAT

DIMENSIONS OF THE TITANIC—CAPACITY—PROVISIONS FOR THE
COMFORT AND ENTERTAINMENT OF PASSENGERS—MECHANICAL
EQUIPMENT—THE ARMY OF ATTENDANTS REQUIRED.

THE statistical record of the great ship gives important
information.

Early in 1908, officials of the White Star Company announced
that they would eclipse all previous records in shipbuilding with
a vessel of staggering dimensions. The Titanic resulted.

The keel of the ill-fated ship was laid in the summer of 1909
at the Harland & Wolff yards, Belfast. Lord Pirrie, considered
one of the best authorities on shipbuilding in the world, was the
designer. The leviathan was launched on May 31, 1911, and was
completed in February, 1912, at a cost of $10,000,000.

SISTER SHIP OF OLYMPIC

The Titanic, largest liner in commission, was a sister ship of
the Olympic. The registered tonnage of each vessel estimated as
45,000, but officers of the White Star Line say that the Titanic
measured 45,328 tons. The Titanic was commanded by Captain
E. J. Smith, the White Star admiral, who had previously been
on the Olympic.

She was 882 ½ feet long, or about four city blocks, and was 5000 tons bigger than a battleship twice as large as the dreadnought Delaware.

Like her sister ship, the Olympic, the Titanic was a four-funneled vessel, and had eleven decks. The distance from the keel to the top of the funnels was 175 feet. She had an average speed of twenty-one knots.

The Titanic could accommodate 2500 passengers. The steamship was divided into numerous compartments, separated by fifteen bulkheads. She was equipped with a gymnasium, swimming pool, hospital with operating room, and a grill and palm garden.

CARRIED CREW OF 860

The registered tonnage was 45,000, and the displacement tonnage 66,000. She was capable of carrying 2500 passengers and the crew numbered 860.

The largest plates employed in the hull were 36 feet long, weighing 4 ½ tons each, and the largest steel beam used was 92 feet long, the weight of this double beam being 4 tons. The rudder, which was operated electrically, weighed 100 tons, the anchors 15 ½ tons each, the center (turbine) propeller 22 tons, and each of the two "wing" propellers 38 tons each. The after "boss-arms," from which were suspended the three propeller shafts, tipped the scales at 73 ½ tons, and the forward "boss-arms" at 45 tons. Each link in the anchor-chains weighed 175 pounds. There were more than 2000 side-lights and windows to light the public rooms and passenger cabins.

Nothing was left to chance in the construction of the Titanic. Three million rivets (weighing 1200 tons) held the solid plates of steel together. To insure stability in binding the heavy plates in the double bottom, half a million rivets, weighing about 270 tons, were used.

All the plating of the hulls was riveted by hydraulic power, driving seven-ton riveting machines, suspended from traveling cranes. The double bottom extended the full length of the vessel, varying from 5 feet 3 inches to 6 feet 3 inches in depth, and lent added strength to the hull.

MOST LUXURIOUS STEAMSHIP

Not only was the Titanic the largest steamship afloat but was the most luxurious. Elaborately furnished cabins opened onto her eleven decks, and some of these decks were reserved as private promenades that were engaged with the best suites. One of these suites was sold for $4350 for the boat's maiden and only voyage. Suites similar, but which were without the private promenade decks, sold for $2300.

The Titanic differed in some respects from her sister ship. The Olympic had a lower promenade deck, but in the Titanic's case the staterooms were brought out flush with the outside of the superstructure, and the rooms themselves made much larger. The sitting rooms of some of the suites on this deck were 15 x 15 feet.

The restaurant was much larger than that of the Olympic and it had a novelty in the shape of a private promenade deck on the starboard side, to be used exclusively by its patrons. Adjoining it was a reception room, where hosts and hostesses could meet their guests.

Two private promenades were connected with the two most luxurious suites on the ship. The suites were situated about amidships, one on either side of the vessel, and each was about 50 feet long. One of the suites comprised a sitting room, two bedrooms and a bath.

These private promenades were expensive luxuries. The cost figured out something like forty dollars a front foot for a six days' voyage. They, with the suites to which they are attached, were the most expensive transatlantic accommodations yet offered.

THE ENGINE ROOM

The engine room was divided into two sections, one given the reciprocating engines and the other to the turbines. There were two sets of the reciprocating kind, one working each of the wing propellers through a four-cylinder triple expansion, direct acting inverted engine. Each set could generate 15,000 indicated horse-power at seventy revolutions a minute. The Parsons type turbine takes steam from the reciprocating engines, and by developing a horse-power of 16,000 at 16.5 revolutions a minute works the third of the ship's propellers, the one directly under the rudder. Of the four funnels of the vessel three were connected with the engine room, and the fourth or after funnel for ventilating the ship including the gallery.

Practically all of the space on the Titanic below the upper deck was occupied by steam-generating plant, coal bunkers and propelling machinery. Eight of the fifteen water-tight compartments contained the mechanical part of the vessel. There were, for instance, twenty-four double end and five single end boilers, each 16 feet 9 inches in diameter, the larger 20 feet long and the smaller 11 feet 9 inches long. The larger boilers had six fires under each of them and the smaller three furnaces. Coal was stored in bunker space along the side of the ship between the lower and middle decks, and was first shipped from there into bunkers running all the way across the vessel in the lowest part. From there the stokers handed it into furnaces.

One of the most interesting features of the vessel was the refrigerating plant, which comprised a huge ice-making and refrigerating machine and a number of provision rooms on the after part of the lower and orlop decks. There were separate cold rooms for beef, mutton, poultry, game, fish, vegetables, fruit, butter, bacon, cheese, flowers, mineral water, wine, spirits and champagne, all maintained at different temperatures most suitable to each. Perishable freight had a compartment its own, also chilled by the plant.

COMFORT AND STABILITY

Two main ideas were carried out in the Titanic. One was comfort and the other stability. The vessel was planned to be an ocean ferry. She was to have only a speed of twenty-one knots, far below that of some other modern vessels, but she was planned to make that speed, blow high or blow low, so that if she left one side of the ocean at a given time she could be relied on to reach the other side at almost a certain minute of a certain hour.

One who has looked into modern methods for safeguarding a vessel of the Titanic type can hardly imagine an accident that could cause her to founder. No collision such as has been the fate of any ship in recent years, it has been thought up to this time, could send her down, nor could running against an iceberg do

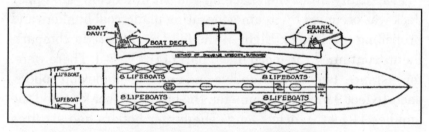

LIFE-BOAT AND DAVITS ON THE TITANIC
This diagram shows very clearly the arrangement of the life-boats and the manner in which they were launched.

it unless such an accident were coupled with the remotely possible blowing out of a boiler. She would sink at once probably, if she were to run over a submerged rock or derelict in such manner that both her keel plates and her double bottom were torn away for more than half her length; but such a catastrophe was so remotely possible that it did not even enter the field of conjecture.

The reason for all this is found in the modern arrangement of water-tight steel compartments into which all ships now are divided and of which the Titanic had fifteen so disposed that half of them, including the largest, could be flooded without impairing the safety of the vessel. Probably it was the working of these bulkheads and the water-tight doors between them as they are supposed to work that saved the Titanic from foundering when she struck the iceberg.

These bulkheads were of heavy sheet steel and started at the very bottom of the ship and extended right up to the top side. The openings in the bulkheads were just about the size of the ordinary doorway, but the doors did not swing as in a house, but fitted into water-tight grooves above the opening. They could be released instantly in several ways, and once closed formed a barrier to the water as solid as the bulkhead itself.

In the Titanic, as in other great modern ships, these doors were held in place above the openings by friction clutches. On the bridge was a switch which connected with an electric magnet at the side of the bulkhead opening. The turning of this switch caused the magnet to draw down a heavy weight, which instantly released the friction clutch, and allowed the door to fall or slide down over the opening in a second. If, however, through accident the bridge switch was rendered useless the doors would close automatically in a few seconds. This was arranged by means of large metal floats at the side of the doorways, which rested just above the level of the double bottom, and as the water entered the compartments these floats would rise to it and directly release the clutch holding the door open. These clutches could also be released by hand.

It was said of the Titanic that her compartments could be flooded as far back or as far forward as the engine room and she would float, though she might take on a heavy list, or settle considerably at one end. To provide against just such an accident as she is said to have encountered she had set back a good distance from the bows an extra heavy cross partition known as the collision bulkhead, which would prevent water getting in amidships, even though a good part of her bow should be torn away. What a ship can stand and still float was shown a few years ago when the Suevic of the White Star Line went on the rocks on the British coast. The wreckers could not move the forward part of her, so they separated her two sections by the use of dynamite, and after putting in a temporary bulkhead floated off the after half of the ship, put it in dry dock and built a new forward part for her. More recently the battleship Maine, or what was left of her, was floated out to sea, and kept on top of the water by her water-tight compartments only.

CHAPTER III

THE MAIDEN VOYAGE OF THE TITANIC

PREPARATIONS FOR THE VOYAGE—SCENES OF GAYETY—THE BOAT SAILS—INCIDENTS OF THE VOYAGE—A COLLISION NARROWLY AVERTED—THE BOAT ON FIRE—WARNED OF ICEBERGS.

NEVER was ill-starred voyage more auspiciously begun than when the Titanic, newly crowned empress of the seas, steamed majestically out of the port of Southampton at noon on Wednesday, April 10th, bound for New York.

Elaborate preparations had been made for the maiden voyage. Crowds of eager watchers gathered to witness the departure, all the more interested because of the notable people who were to travel aboard her. Friends and relatives of many of the passengers were at the dock to bid Godspeed to their departing loved ones. The passengers themselves were unusually gay and happy.

Majestic and beautiful the ship rested on the water, a marvel of shipbuilding, worthy of any sea. As this new queen of the ocean moved slowly from her dock, no one questioned her construction: she was fitted with an elaborate system of water-tight compartments, calculated to make her unsinkable; she had been pronounced the safest as well as the most sumptuous Atlantic liner afloat.

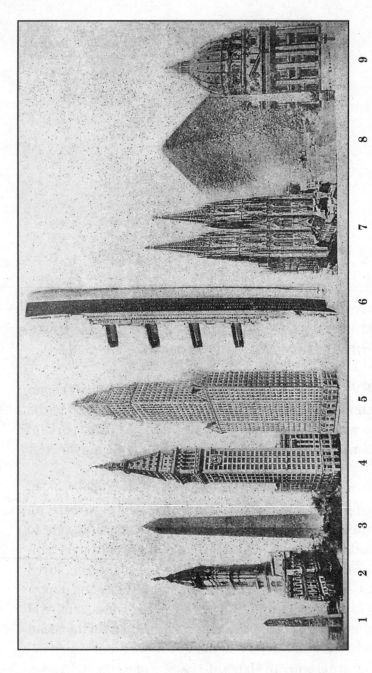

STEAMER "TITANIC" COMPARED WITH THE LARGEST STRUCTURES IN THE WORLD

1. Bunker Hill Monument, Boston, 221 feet high.   2. Public Buildings, Philadelphia, 534 feet high.   3. Washington Monument, Washington, 555 feet high.   4. Metropolitan Tower, New York, 700 feet high.   5. Woolworth Building, New York, 750 feet high.   6. Steamer "Titanic," White Star Line, 882 ½ feet long.   7. Cologne Cathedral, Cologne, Germany, 516 feet high.   8. Grand Pyramid, Gizeh, Africa, 451 feet high.   9. St. Peter's Church, Rome, Italy, 448 feet high.

There was silence just before the boat pulled out—the silence that usually precedes the leave-taking. The heavy whistles sounded and the splendid Titanic, her flags flying and her band playing, churned the water and plowed heavily away.

Then the Titanic, with the people on board waving handkerchiefs and shouting good-byes that could be heard only as a buzzing murmur on shore, rode away on the ocean, proudly, majestically, her head up and, so it seemed, her shoulders thrown back. If ever a vessel seemed to throb with proud life, if ever a monster of the sea seemed to "feel its oats" and strain at the leash, if ever a ship seemed to have breeding and blue blood that would keep it going until its heart broke, that ship was the Titanic.

And so it was only her due that as the Titanic steamed out of the harbor bound on her maiden voyage a thousand "God-speeds" were wafted after her, while every other vessel that she passed, the greatest of them dwarfed by her colossal proportions, paid homage to the new queen regnant with the blasts of their whistles and the shrieking of steam sirens.

THE SHIP'S CAPTAIN

In command of the Titanic was Captain E J. Smith, a veteran of the seas, and admiral of the White Star Line fleet. The next six officers, in the order of their rank, were Murdock, Lightoller, Pitman, Boxhall, Lowe and Moody. Dan Phillips was chief wireless operator, with Harold Bride as assistant.

From the forward bridge, fully ninety feet above the sea, peered out the benign face of the ship's master, cool of aspect, deliberate of action, impressive in that quality of confidence that is bred only of long experience in command.

From far below the bridge sounded the strains of the ship's orchestra, playing blithely a favorite air from "The Chocolate Soldier." All went as merry as a wedding bell Indeed, among that gay ship's company were two score or more at least for whom the wedding bells had sounded in truth not many days before. Some were on their honeymoon tours, others were returning to their motherland after having passed the weeks of the honey-

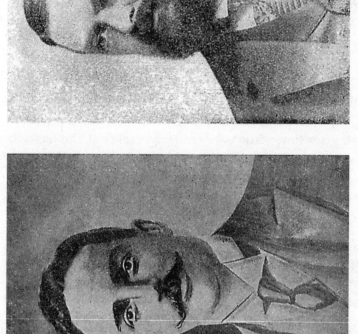

J. BRUCE ISMAY

Managing director of the International Mercantile Marine, and managing director of the White Star Line. Mr. Ismay had made it a custom to be a passenger on the maiden voyage of every new ship built by the company.

CHARLES M. HAYS

President of the Grand Trunk and Grand Trunk Pacific Railways, numbered among the heroic men who willingly stood back to make room for women and children in the life-boats of the Titanic.

moon, like Colonel John Jacob Astor and his young bride, amid the diversions of Egypt or other Old World countries.

What daring flight of imagination would have ventured the prediction that within the span of six days that stately ship, humbled, shattered and torn asunder, would lie two thousand fathoms deep at the bottom of the Atlantic, that the benign face that peered from the bridge would be set in the rigor of death and that the happy bevy of voyaging brides would be sorrowing widows?

ALMOST IN A COLLISION

The big vessel had, however, a touch of evil fortune before she cleared the harbor of Southampton. As she passed down stream her immense bulk—she displaced 66,000 tons-drew the waters after her with an irresistible suction that tore the American liner New York from her moorings; seven steel hawsers were snapped like twine. The New York floated toward the White Star ship, and would have rammed the new ship had not the tugs Vulcan and Neptune stopped her and towed her back to the quay.

When the mammoth ship touched at Cherbourg and later at Queenstown she was again the object of a port ovation, the smaller craft doing obeisance while thousands gazed in wonder at her stupendous proportions. After taking aboard some additional passengers at each port, the Titanic headed her towering bow toward the open sea and the race for a record on her maiden voyage was begun.

NEW BURST OF SPEED EACH DAY

The Titanic made 484 miles as her first day's run, her powerful new engines turning over at the rate of seventy revolutions. On the second day out the speed was hit up to seventy-three revolutions and the run for the day was bulletined as 519 miles. Still further increasing the speed, the rate of revolution of the engines was raised to seventy-five and the day's run was 549 miles, the best yet scheduled.

But the ship had not yet been speeded to her capacity; she

was capable of turning over about seventy-eight revolutions. Had the weather conditions been propitious, it was intended to press the great racer to he full limit of her speed on Monday. But for the Titanic, Monday never came.

FIRE IN THE COAL BUNKERS

Unknown to the passengers, the Titanic was on fire from the day she sailed from Southampton. Her officers and crew knew it, for they had fought the fire for days.

This story, told for the first time by the survivors of the crew, was only one of the many thrilling tales of the fateful first voyage.

"The Titanic sailed from Southampton on Wednesday; April 10th, at noon," said J. Dilley, fireman on the Titanic.

"I was assigned to the Titanic from the Oceanic, where I had served as a fireman. From the day we sailed the Titanic was on fire, and my sole duty, together with eleven other men, had been to fight that fire. We had made no headway against it."

PASSENGERS IN IGNORANCE

"Of course," he went on, "the passengers knew nothing of the fire. Do you think we'd have let them know about it? No, sir.

"The fire started in bunker No. 6. There were hundreds of tons of coal stored there. The coal on top of the bunker was wet, as all the coal should have been, but down at the bottom of the bunker the coal had been permitted to get dry.

"The dry coal at the bottom of the pile took fire, and smouldered for days. The wet coal on top kept the flames from coming through, but down in the bottom of the bunkers the flames were raging.

"Two men from each watch of stokers were tolled off, to fight that fire. The stokers worked four hours at a time, so twelve of us were fighting flames from the day we put out of Southampton until we hit the iceberg.

"No, we didn't get that fire out, and among the stokers there was talk that we'd have to empty the big coal bunkers after we'd put our passengers off in New York, and then call on the fire-boats there to help us put out the fire.

"The stokers were alarmed over it, but the officers told us to keep our mouths shut—they didn't want to alarm the passengers."

USUAL DIVERSION

Until Sunday, April 14th, then, the voyage had apparently been a delightful but uneventful one. The passengers had passed the time in the usual diversions of ocean travelers, amusing themselves in the luxurious saloons, promenading on the boat deck, lolling at their ease in steamer chairs and making pools on the daily runs of the steamship. The smoking rooms and card rooms had been as well patronized as usual, and a party of several notorious professional gamblers had begun reaping their usual easy harvest.

As early as Sunday afternoon the officers of the Titanic must have known that they were approaching dangerous ice fields of the kind that are a perennial menace to the safety of steamships following the regular transatlantic lanes off the Great Banks of Newfoundland.

AN UNHEEDED WARNING

On Sunday afternoon the Titanic's wireless operator forwarded to the Hydrographic office in Washington, Baltimore, Philadelphia and elsewhere the following dispatch:

"April 14.—The German steamship Amerika (Hamburg-American Line) reports by radio-telegraph passing two large icebergs in latitude 41.27, longitude 50.08.—Titanic, Br. S. S."

Despite this warning, the Titanic forged ahead Sunday night at her usual speed—from twenty-one to twenty-five knots.

CHAPTER IV

SOME OF THE NOTABLE PASSENGERS

SKETCHES OF PROMINENT MEN AND WOMEN ON BOARD, INCLUD-
ING MAJOR ARCHIBALD BUTT, JOHN JACOB ASTOR, BENJAMIN
GUGGENHEIM, ISIDOR STRAUS, J. BRUCE ISMAY, GEORGE D.
WIDENER, COLONEL WASHINGTON ROEBLING, 2D, CHARLES M. HAYS,
W. T. STEAD AND OTHERS.

THE ship's company was of a character befitting the
greatest of all vessels and worthy of the occasion of her
maiden voyage. Though the major part of her passengers were Americans returning from abroad, there were enrolled
upon her cabin lists some of the most distinguished names of
England, as well as of the younger nation. Many of these had pur-
posely delayed sailing, or had hastened their departure, that they
might be among the first passengers on the great vessel.

There were aboard six men whose fortunes ran into tens of
millions, besides many other persons of international note.
Among the men were leaders in the world of commerce, finance,
literature, art and the learned professions. Many of the women
were socially prominent in two hemispheres.

Wealth and fame, unfortunately, are not proof against fate,
and most of these notable personages perished as pitiably as the
more humble steerage passengers.

The list of notables included Colonel John Jacob Astor, head of the Astor family, whose fortune is estimated at $150,000,000; Isidor Straus, merchant and banker ($50,000,000); J. Bruce Ismay, managing director of the International Mercantile Marine ($40,000,000); Benjamin Guggenheim, head of the Guggenheim family ($95,000,000); George D. Widener, son of P. A. B. Widener, traction magnate and financier ($5,000,000); Colonel Washington Roebling, builder of the great Brooklyn Bridge; Charles M. Hays, president of the Grand Trunk Railway; W. T. Stead, famous publicist; Jacques Futrelle, journalist; Henry S. Harper, of the firm of Harper & Bros.; Henry B. Harris, theatrical manager; Major Archibald Butt, military aide to President Taft; and Francis D. Millet, one of the best known American painters.

MAJOR BUTT

Major Archibald Butt, whose bravery on the sinking vessel will not soon be forgotten, was military aide to President Taft and was known wherever the President traveled. His recent European mission was apparently to call on the Pope in behalf of President Taft; for on March 21st he was received at the Vatican, and presented to the Pope a letter from Mr. Taft thanking the Pontiff for the creation of three new American Cardinals.

Major Butt had a reputation as a horseman, and it is said he was able to keep up with President Roosevelt, be the ride ever so far or fast. He was promoted to the rank of major in 1911. He sailed for the Mediterranean on March 2d with his friend Francis D. Millet, the artist, who also perished on the Titanic.

COLONEL ASTOR

John Jacob Astor was returning from a trip to Egypt with his nineteen-year-old bride, formerly Miss Madeline Force, to whom he was married in Providence, September 9, 1911. He was head of the family whose name he bore and one of the world's wealthiest men. He was not, however, one of the world's "idle rich," for his life of forty-seven years was a well-filled one. He had managed the family estates since 1891; built the Astor Hotel, New York; was colonel on the staff of Governor Levi P. Morton, and in May, 1898, was commissioned colonel of the United States volunteers. After assisting Major General Breckinridge, inspector-general of the United States army, he was assigned to duty on the staff of Major-General Shafter and served in Cuba during the operations ending in the surrender of Santiago. He was also the inventor of a bicycle brake, a pneumatic road-improver, and an improved turbine engine.

BENJAMIN GUGGENHEIM

Next to Colonel Astor in financial importance was Benjamin Guggenheim, whose father founded the famous house of M. Guggenheim and Sons. When the various Guggenheim interests were consolidated into the American Smelt and Refining Company he retired from active business, although he later became interested in the Power and Mining Machinery Company of Milwaukee. In 1894 he married Miss Floretta Seligman, daughter of James Seligman, the New York banker.

ISIDOR STRAUS

Isidor Straus, whose wife elected to perish with him in the ship, was a brother of Nathan and Oscar Straus, a partner with Nathan Straus in R. H. Macy & Co. and L Straus, & Sons, a member of the firm of Abraham & Straus in Brooklyn, and has been well known in politics and charitable work. He was a member of the Fifty-third Congress from 1893 to 1895, and as a friend of William L. Wilson was in constant consultation in the matter of the former Wilson tariff bill.

Mr. Straus was conspicuous for his works of charity and was an ardent supporter of every enterprise to improve the condition of the Hebrew immigrants. He was president of the Educational Alliance, vice-president of the J. Hood Wright Memorial Hospital, a member of the Chamber of Commerce, on one of the visiting

ACTUAL PHOTOGRAPH OF THE ICEBERG THAT SUNK THE TITANIC

Lady Duff Gordon, a prominent English woman who was aboard the Titanic, on landing in New York told how she had seen the iceberg a few minutes before the Titanic ran into it. "We had watched for some time the field of ice," said Lady Gordon, "and noticed a number of large bergs. This was one which one of the officers pointed out to me. He said that it must be one hundred feet high and seemed to be a mile long. It was away off in the distance.

HEART-BREAKING FAREWELLS

Both men and women were loaded into the first boats, but soon the cry of "Women first" was raised. Then came the real note of tragedy. Husbands and wives clung to each other in farewell; some refused to be separated.

committees of Harvard University, and was besides a trustee of many financial and philanthropic institutions.

Mr. Straus never enjoyed a college education. He was however, one of the best informed men of the day, his information having been derived from extensive reading. His library, said to be one of the finest and most extensive in New York, was his pride and his place of special recreation.

GEORGE D. WIDENER

The best known of Philadelphia passengers aboard the Titanic were Mr. and Mrs. George D. Widener. Mr. Widener was a son of Peter A. B. Widener and, like his father, was recognized as one of the foremost financiers of Philadelphia as well as a leader in society there. Mr. Widener married Miss Eleanor Elkins, a daughter of the late William L. Elkins. They made their home with his father at the latter's fine place at Eastbourne, ten miles from Philadelphia. Mr. Widener was keenly interested in horses and was a constant exhibitor at horse shows. In business he was recognized as his father's chief adviser in managing the latter's extensive traction interests. P. A. B. Widener is a director of the International Mercantile Marine.

Mrs. Widener is said to be the possessor of one of the finest collections of jewels in the world, the gift of her husband. One string of pearls in this collection was reported to be worth $250,000.

The Wideners went abroad two months previous to disaster, Mr. Widener desiring to inspect some of his business interests on the other side. At the opening of the London Museum by King George on March 21st last it was announced that Mrs. Widener had presented to the museum thirty silver plates once the property of Nell Gwyn. Mr. Widener is survived by a daughter, Eleanor, and a son, George D. Widener, Jr. Harry Elkins Widener was with his parents and went down on the ship.

COLONEL ROEBLING

Colonel Washington Augustus Roebling was president of the John A. Roebling Sons' Company, manufacturers of iron and steel wire rope. He served in the Union Army from 1861 to 1865, resigning to assist his father in the construction of the Cincinnati and Covington suspension bridge. At the death of his father in 1869 he took entire charge of the construction of the Brooklyn Bridge, and it is to his genius that the success of that great work may be said to be due.

WILLIAM T. STEAD

One of the most notable of the foreign passengers was William T. Stead. Few names are more widely known to the world of contemporary literature and journalism than that of the brilliant editor of the Review of Reviews. Matthew Arnold called him "the inventor of the new journalism in England." He was on his way to America to take part in the Men and Religion Forward Movement and was to have delivered an address in Union Square on the Thursday after the disaster, with William Jennings Bryan as his chief associate.

Mr. Stead was an earnest advocate of peace and had written many books. His commentary "If Christ Came to Chicago" raised a storm twenty years ago. When he was in this country in 1907 he addressed a session of Methodist clergymen, and at one juncture of the meeting remarked that unless the Methodists did something about the peace movement besides shouting "amen" nobody "would care a damn about their amens!"

OTHER ENGLISHMEN ABOARD

Other distinguished Englishmen on the Titanic were Norman C. Craig, M.P., Thomas Andrews, a representative of the firm of Harland & Wolff, of Belfast, the ship's builders, and J. Bruce Ismay, managing director of the White Star Line.

J. BRUCE ISMAY

Mr. Ismay is president and one of the founders of the International Mercantile Marine. He has made it a custom to be a passenger on the maiden voyage of every new ship built by the White Star Line. It was Mr. Ismay who, with J. P. Morgan, consolidated the British steamship lines under the International Mercantile Marine's control; and it is largely due to his imagination that such gigantic ships as the Titanic and Olympic were made possible.

JACQUES FUTRELLE

Jacques Futrelle was an author of short stories, some of which have appeared in the Saturday Evening Post, and of many novels of the same general type as "The Thinking Machine," with which he first gained a wide popularity. Newspaper work, chiefly in Richmond, Va., engaged his attention from 1890 to 1902, in which year he entered the theatrical business as a manager. In 1904 he returned to his journalistic career.

HENRY B. HARRIS

Henry B. Harris, the theater manager, had been manager of May Irwin, Peter Dailey, Lily Langtry, Amelia Bingham, and launched Robert Edeson as star. He became the manager of the Hudson Theater in 1903 and the Hackett Theater in 1906. Among his best known productions are "The Lion and the Mouse," "The Traveling Salesman" and "The Third Degree." He was president of the Henry B. Harris Company controlling the Harris Theater.

Young Harris had a liking for the theatrical business from a boy. Twelve years ago Mr. Harris married Miss Rene Wallach of Washington. He was said to have a fortune of between $1,000,000 and $3,000,000. He owned outright the Hudson and the Harris theaters and had an interest in two other show houses in New York. He owned three theaters in Chicago, one in Syracuse and one in Philadelphia.

HENRY S. HARPER

Henry Sleeper Harper, who was among the survivors, is a grandson of John Wesley Harper, one of the founders of the Harper publishing business. H. Sleeper Harper was himself an incorporator of Harper & Brothers when the firm became a corporation in 1896. He had a desk in the offices of the publishers, but his hand of late years in the management of the business has been very slight. He has been active in the work of keeping the Adirondack forests free from aggression. He was in the habit of spending about half of his time in foreign travel. His friends in New York recalled that he had a narrow escape about ten years ago when a ship in which he was traveling ran into an iceberg on the Grand Banks.

FRANCIS DAVID MILLET

Millet was one of the best-known American painters and many of his canvasses are found in the leading galleries of the world. He served as a drummer boy with the Sixtieth Massachusetts volunteers in the Civil War, and from early manhood took a prominent part in public affairs. He was director of the decorations for the Chicago Exposition and was, at the time of the disaster, secretary of the American Academy in Rome. He was a wide traveler and the author of many books, besides translations of Tolstoy.

CHARLES M. HAYS

Another person of prominence was Charles Melville Hays, president of the Grand Trunk and the Grand Trunk Pacific railways. He was described by Sir Wilfrid Laurier at a dinner of the Canadian Club of New York, at the Hotel Astor last year, as "beyond question the greatest railroad genius in Canada, as an executive genius ranking second only to the late Edward H. Harriman." He was returning aboard the Titanic with his wife and son-in-law and daughter, Mr. and Mrs. Thornton Davidson, of Montreal.

CHAPTER V

THE TITANIC STRIKES AN ICEBERG!

TARDY ATTENTION TO WARNING RESPONSIBLE FOR ACCIDENT—
THE DANGER NOT REALIZED AT FIRST—AN INTERRUPTED CARD
GAME—PASSENGERS JOKE AMONG THEMSELVES—THE REAL
TRUTH DAWNS—PANIC ON BOARD—WIRELESS CALLS FOR HELP.

SUNDAY night the magnificent ocean liner was plunging
through a comparatively placid sea, on the surface of which
there was much mushy ice and here and there a number
of comparatively harmless-looking floes. The night was clear and
stars visible. First Officer William T. Murdock was in charge of
the bridge. The first intimation of the presence of the iceberg that
he received was from the lookout in the crow's nest.

Three warnings were transmitted from the crow's nest of the
Titanic to the officer on the doomed steamship's bridge 15 minutes before she struck, according to Thomas Whiteley, a first
saloon steward.

Whiteley, who was whipped overboard from the ship by a rope
while helping to lower a life-boat, finally reported on the
Carpathia aboard one of the boats that contained, he said, both
the crow's nest lookouts. He heard a conversation between them,
he asserted, in which they discussed the warnings given to the
Titanic's bridge of the presence of the iceberg.

Whiteley did not know the names of either of the lookout men and believed that they returned to England with the majority of the surviving members of the crew.

"I heard one of them say that at 11.15 o'clock, 15 minutes before the Titanic struck, he had reported to First Officer Murdock, on the bridge, that he fancied he saw an iceberg," said Whiteley.

A GRAPHIC ILLUSTRATION OF THE FORCE WITH WHICH A VESSEL STRIKES AN ICEBERG

"Twice after that, the lookout said, he warned Murdock that a berg was ahead. They were very indignant that no attention was paid to their warnings."

TARDY ATTENTION TO WARNING RESPONSIBLE FOR ACCIDENT

Murdock's tardy answering of a telephone call from the crow's nest is assigned by Whiteley as the cause of the disaster.

When Murdock answered the call he received the information that the iceberg was due ahead. This information was imparted just a few seconds before the crash, and had the officer promptly answered the ring of the bell it is probable that the accident could have been avoided, or at least, been reduced by the lowered speed.

The lookout saw a towering "blue berg" looming up in the sea path of the Titanic, and called the bridge on the ship's telephone. When, after the passing of those two or three fateful minutes an officer on the bridge lifted the telephone receiver from its hook to answer the lookout, it was too late. The speeding liner, cleaving a calm sea under a star-studded sky, had reached the floating mountain of ice, which the theoretically "unsinkable" ship struck a crashing, if glancing, blow with her starboard bow.

MURDOCK PAID WITH LIFE

Had Murdock, according to the account of the tragedy given by two of the Titanic's seamen, known how imperative was that call from the lookout man, the men at the wheel of the liner might have swerved the great ship sufficiently to avoid the berg altogether. At the worst the vessel would probably have struck the mass of ice with her stern

Murdock if the tale of the Titanic sailor be true, expiated his negligence by shooting himself within sight of all alleged victims huddled in life-boats or struggling in the icy seas.

When at last the danger was realized, the great ship was so close upon the berg that it was practically impossible to avoid collision with it.

VAIN TRIAL TO CLEAR BERG

The first officer did what other startled and alert commanders would have done under similar circumstances, that is, he made an effort by going full speed ahead on the starboard propeller and reversing his port propeller, simultaneously throwing his helm over, to make a rapid turn and clear the berg. The maneuver was not successful. He succeed in saving his bows from crashing into the ice-cliff, but nearly the entire length of the underbody of the great ship on the starboard side was ripped. The speed of the Titanic, estimated to be at least twenty-one knots, was so terrific that the knife-like edge of the iceberg's spur protruding under the sea cut through her like a can-opener.

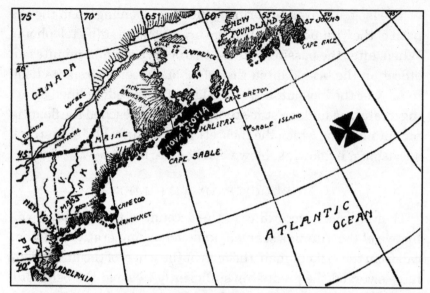

THE LOCATION OF THE DISASTER

The Titanic was in 41.46 north latitude and 50.14 west longitude when she was struck, very near the spot on the wide Atlantic where the Carmania encountered a field of ice, studded with great bergs, on her voyage to New York which ended on April 14th. It was really an ice pack, due to an unusually severe winter in the north Atlantic. No less than twenty-five bergs, some of great height, were counted.

The shock was almost imperceptible. The first officer did not apparently realize that the great ship had received her death wound, and none of the passengers had the slightest suspicion that anything more than a usual minor sea accident had happened. Hundreds who had gone to their berths and were asleep were unawakened by the vibration.

BRIDGE GAME NOT DISTURBED

To illustrate the placidity with which practically all the men regarded the accident it is related that Pierre Maréchal, son of the vice-admiral of the French navy, Lucien Smith, Paul Chevré, a French sculptor, and A. F. Ormont, a cotton broker, were in the Café Parisien playing bridge.

The four calmly got up from the table and after walking on deck and looking over the rail returned to their game. One of them had left his cigar on the card table, and while the three others were gazing out on the sea he remarked that he couldn't afford to lose his smoke, returned for his cigar and came out again.

They remained only for a few moments on deck, and then resumed their game under the impression that the ship had stopped for reasons best known to the captain and not involving any danger to her. Later, in describing the scene that took place, M. Maréchal, who was among the survivors, said: "When three-quarters of a mile away we stopped, the spectacle before our eyes was in its way magnificent. In a very calm sea, beneath a sky moonless but sown with millions of stars, the enormous Titanic lay on the water, illuminated from the water line to the boat deck. The bow was slowly sinking into the black water."

The tendency of the whole ship's company except the men in the engine department, who were made aware of the danger by the inrushing water, was to make light of and in some instances even to ridicule the thought of danger to so substantial a fabric.

THE CAPTAIN ON DECK

When Captain Smith came from the chart room onto the bridge, his first words were, "Close the emergency doors."

"They're already closed, sir," Mr. Murdock replied.

"Send to the carpenter and tell him to sound the ship," was the next order. The message was sent to the carpenter, but the carpenter never came up to report. He was probably the first man on the ship to lose his life.

The captain then looked at the communicator, which shows in what direction the ship is listing. He saw that she carried five degrees list to starboard.

The ship was then rapidly settling forward. All the steam sirens were blowing. By the captain's orders, given in the next few minutes, the engines were put to work at pumping out the ship, distress signals were sent by the Marconi, and rockets were sent up from the bridge by Quartermaster Rowe. All hands were ordered on deck.

PASSENGERS NOT ALARMED

The blasting shriek of the sirens had not alarmed the great company of the Titanic, because such steam calls are an incident of travel in seas where fogs roll. Many had gone to bed, but the hour, 11.40 P. M., was not too late for the friendly contact of saloons and smoking rooms. It was Sunday night and the ship's concert had ended, but there were many hundreds up and moving among the gay lights, and many on deck with their eyes strained toward the mysterious west, where home lay. And in one jarring, breath-sweeping moment all of these, asleep or awake, were at the mercy of chance. Few among the more than 2000 aboard could have had a thought of danger. The man who had stood up in the smoking room to say that the Titanic was vulnerable or that in a few minutes two-thirds of her people would be face to face with death, would have been considered a fool or a lunatic. No ship ever sailed the seas that gave her passengers more confidence, more cool security.

Within a few minutes stewards and other members of the crew were sent round to arouse the people. Some utterly refused to get up. The stewards had almost to force the doors of the staterooms to make the somnolent appreciate their peril, and many of them, it is believed, were drowned like rats in a trap.

ASTOR AND WIFE STROLLED ON DECK

Colonel and Mrs. Astor were in their room and saw the ice vision flash by. They had not appreciably felt the gentle shock and supposed that nothing out of the ordinary had happened. They were both dressed and came on deck leisurely. William T.

Stead, the London journalist, wandered on deck for a few minutes, stopping to talk to Frank Millet. "What do they say is the trouble?" he asked. "Icebergs," was the brief reply. "Well," said Stead, "I guess it is nothing serious. I'm going back to my cabin to read."

From end to end on the mighty boat officers were rushing about without much noise or confusion, but giving orders sharply. Captain Smith told the third officer to rush downstairs and see whether the water was coming in very fast. "And," he added, "take some armed guards along to see that the stokers and engineers stay at their posts."

In two minutes the officer returned. "It looks pretty bad, sir," he said. "The water is rushing in and filling the bottom. The locks of the water-tight compartments have been sprung by the shock."

"Give the command for all passengers to be on deck with life-belts on."

Through the length and breadth of the boat, upstairs and downstairs, on all decks, the cry rang out: "All passengers on deck with life-preservers."

A SUDDEN TREMOR OF FEAR

For the first time, there was a feeling of panic. Husbands sought for wives and children. Families gathered together. Many who were asleep hastily caught up their clothing and rushed on deck. A moment before the men had been joking about the life-belts, according to the story told by Mrs. Vera Dick, of Calgary, Canada. "Try this one," one man said to her, "they are the very latest thing this season. Everybody's wearing them now."

Another man suggested to a woman friend, who had a fox terrier in her arms, that she should put a life-saver on the dog. "It won't fit," the woman replied, laughing. "Make him carry it in his mouth," said the friend.

CONFUSION ON STERRAGE DECK

Below, on the steerage deck, there was intense confusion. About the time the officers on the first deck gave the order that all men should stand to one side and all women should go below to deck B, taking the children with them, a similar order was given to the steerage passengers. The women were ordered to the front, the men to the rear. Half a dozen healthy, husky men pushed their way forward and tried to crowd into the first boat.

"Stand back," shouted the officers who were manning the boat. "The women come first."

Shouting curses in various languages, the men continued their pushing and tugging to climb into the boats. Shots rang out. One big fellow fell over the railing into the water. Another dropped to the deck, moaning. His jaw had been shot away. This was the story told by the bystanders afterwards on the pier. One eye-witness told the writer on the pier that the way in which the men were shot down was horrible. His sympathy was with the men who were shot.

"They were only trying to save their lives," he said.

WIRELESS OPERATOR DIED AT HIS POST

On board the Titanic, the wireless operator, with a life-belt about his waist, was hitting the instrument that was sending out C. Q. D. messages, "Struck on iceberg, C. Q. D."

"Shall I tell captain to turn back and help?" flashed a reply from the Carpathia.

"Yes, old man," the Titanic wireless operator responded. "Guess we're sinking."

An hour later, when the second wireless man came into the boxlike room to tell his companion what the situation was, he found a stoker creeping up behind the operator and saw him raise a knife over his head. He said afterwards—he was among those rescued—that he realized at once that the stoker intended to kill the operator in order to take his life-belt from him. The second operator pulled out his revolver and shot the stoker dead.

"What was the trouble?" asked the operator.

"That man was going to kill you and steal your life-belt," the second man replied.

"Thanks, old man," said the operator. The second man went on deck to get some more information. He was just in time to jump overboard before the Titanic went down. The wireless operator and the body of the stoker who tried to steal his belt went down together.

On the deck where the first class passengers were quartered, known as deck A, there was none of the confusion that was taking place on the lower decks. The Titanic was standing without much rocking. The captain had given an order and the band was playing.

WAITING FOR THE NEWS

A bird's-eye view of the great crowds outside of the White Star Line Office in New York, seeking news of the Titanic. The insert shows Mrs. Benjamin Guggenheim, the wife of the smelter millionaire, leaving the steamship office after inquiry for news of her husband who was aboard the ill-fated steamship. On the left are Mr. and Mrs. Dewitt Seligman, who accompanied Mrs. Guggenheim.

CHAPTER VI

"WOMEN AND CHILDREN FIRST!"

COOL-HEADED OFFICERS AND CREW BRING ORDER OUT OF
CHAOS—FILLING THE LIFE-BOATS—HEARTRENDING SCENES AS
FAMILIES ARE PARTED—FOUR LIFE-BOATS LOST—INCIDENTS OF
BRAVERY—"THE BOATS ARE ALL FILLED!"

ONCE on the deck, many hesitated to enter the swinging life-boats. The glassy sea, the starlit sky, the absence, in the first few moments, of intense excitement, gave them the feeling that there was only some slight mishap; that those who got into the boats would have a chilly half hour below and might, later, be laughed at.

It was such a feeling as this, from all accounts, which caused John Jacob Astor and his wife to refuse the places offered them in the first boat, and to retire to the gymnasium. In the same way H. J. Allison, a Montreal banker, laughed at the warning, and his wife, reassured by him, took her time dressing. They and their daughter did not reach the Carpathia. Their son, less than two years old, was carried into a life-boat by his nurse, and was taken in charge by Major Arthur Peuchen.

THE LIFE-BOATS LOWERED

The admiration felt by the passengers and crew for the matchlessly appointed vessel was translated, in those first few moments, into a confidence which for some proved deadly. The

WIRELESS STATION AT CAPE RACE
Where the first news of the Titanic disaster was received.

pulsing of the engines had ceased, and the steamship lay just as though she were awaiting the order to go on again after some trifling matter had been adjusted. But in a few minutes the canvas covers were lifted from the life-boats and the crews allotted to each standing by, ready to lower them to the water.

Nearly all the boats that were lowered on the port side of the ship touched the water without capsizing. Four of the others lowered to starboard, including one collapsible, were capsized. All, however, who were in the collapsible boats that practically went to pieces, were rescued by the other boats.

Presently the order was heard: "All men stand back and all women retire to the deck below." That was the smokingroom deck, or the B deck. The men stood away and remained in absolute silence, leaning against the rail or pacing up and down the deck slowly. Many of them lighted cigars or cigarettes and began to smoke.

LOADING THE BOATS

The boats were swung out and lowered from the A deck above. The women were marshaled quietly in lines along the B deck, and when the boats were lowered down to the level of the latter the women were assisted to climb into them.

As each of the boats was filled with its quota of passengers the word was given and it was carefully lowered down to the dark surface of the water.

Nobody seemed to know how Mr. Ismay got into a boat, but it was assumed that he wished to make a presentation of the case of the Titanic to his company. He was among those who apparently realized that the splendid ship was doomed. All hands in the life-boats, under instructions from officers and men in charge, were rowed a considerable distance from the ship herself in order to get far away from the possible suction that would follow her foundering.

COOLEST MEN ON BOARD

Captain Smith and Major Archibald Butt, military aide to the President of the United States, were among the coolest men on board. A number of steerage passengers were yelling and screaming and fighting to get to the boats. Officers drew guns and told them that if they moved towards the boats they would be shot dead. Major Butt had a gun in his hand and covered the men who tried to get to the boats.

The following story of his bravery was told by Mrs. Henry B. Harris, wife of the theatrical manager:

"The world should rise in praise of Major Butt. That man's conduct will remain in my memory forever. The American army is honored by him and the way he taught some of the other men how to behave when women and children were suffering that awful mental fear of death. Major Butt was near me and I noticed everything that he did.

"When the order to man the boats came, the captain whispered something to Major Butt. The two of them had become friends. The major immediately became as one in supreme command. You would have thought he was at a White House reception. A dozen or more women became hysterical all at once, as something connected with a life-boat went wrong. Major Butt stepped over to them and said:

" 'Really, you must not act like that, we are all going to see you through this thing.' He helped the sailors rearrange the rope or chain that had gone wrong and lifted some of the women in with a touch of gallantry. Not only was there a complete lack of any fear in his manner, but there was the action of an aristocrat.

"When the time came he was a man to be feared. In one of the earlier boats fifty women, it seemed, were about to be lowered, when a man, suddenly panic-stricken, ran to the stern of it. Major Butt shot one arm out, caught him by the back of the neck and jerked him backward like a pillow. His head cracked against a rail and he was stunned.

" 'Sorry,' said Major Butt, 'women will be attended to first or I'll break every damned bone in your body.'

FORCED MEN USURPING PLACES TO VACATE

"The boats were lowered one by one, and as I stood by, my husband said to me, 'Thank God for Archie Butt.' Perhaps Major Butt heard it, for he turned his face towards us for a second and smiled. Just at that moment, a young man was arguing to get into a life-boat, and Major Butt had a hold of the lad by the arm, like a big brother, and was telling him to keep his head and be a man.

"Major Butt helped those poor frightened steerage people so wonderfully, so tenderly and yet with such cool and manly firmness that he prevented the loss of many lives from panic. He was a soldier to the last. He was one of God's greatest noblemen, and I think I can say he was an example of bravery even to men on the ship."

LAST WORDS OF MAJOR BUTT

Miss Marie Young, who was a music instructor to President Roosevelt's children and had known Major Butt during the Roosevelt occupancy of the White House, told this story of his heroism.

"Archie himself put me into the boat, wrapped blankets about me and tucked me in as carefully as if we were starting on a motor ride. He, himself, entered the boat with me, performing the little courtesies as calmly and with as smiling a face as if death were far away, instead of being but a few moments removed from him.

"When he had carefully wrapped me up he stepped upon the gunwale of the boat, and lifting his hat, smiled down at me. 'Goodbye, Miss Young,' he said. 'Good luck to you, and don't forget to remember me to the folks back home.' Then he stepped back and waved his hand to me as the boat was lowered. I think I was the last woman he had a chance to help, for the boat went down shortly after we cleared the suction zone."

COLONEL ASTOR ANOTHER HERO

Colonel Astor was another of the heroes of the awful night. Effort was made to persuade him to take a place in one of the life-boats, but he emphatically refused to do so until every woman and child on board had been provided for, not excepting the women members of the ship's company.

One of the passengers describing the consummate courage of Colonel Astor said:

"He led Mrs. Astor to the side of the ship and helped her to the life-boat to which she had been assigned. I saw that she was prostrated and said she would remain and take her chances with him, but Colonel Astor quietly insisted and tried to reassure her in a few words. As she took her place in the boat her eyes were fixed upon him. Colonel Astor smiled, touched his cap, and when the boat moved safely away from the ship's side he turned back to his place among the men."

Mrs. Ida S. Hippach and her daughter Jean, survivors of the Titanic, said they were saved by Colonel John Jacob Astor, who forced the crew of the last life-boat to wait for them.

"We saw Colonel Astor place Mrs. Astor in a boat and assure her that he would follow later," said Mrs. Hippach.

"He turned to us with a smile and said, 'Ladies, you are next.' The officer in charge of the boat protested that the craft was full, and the seamen started to lower it.

"Colonel Astor exclaimed, 'Hold that boat,' in the voice of a man accustomed to be obeyed, and they did as he ordered. The boat had been lowered past the upper deck and the colonel took us to the deck below and put us in the boat, one after the other, through a port-hole."

HEART-BREAKING SCENES

There were some terrible scenes. Fathers were parting from their children and giving them an encouraging pat on the shoulders; men were kissing their wives and telling them that they would be with them shortly. One man said there was absolutely no danger, that the boat was the finest ever built, with water-tight compartments, and that it could not sink. That seemed to be the general impression.

THE NATURE OF THE INJURY SUSTAINED BY THE TITANIC

A few of the men, however, were panic-stricken even when the first of the fifty-six foot life-boats was being filled. Fully ten men threw themselves into the boats already crowded with women and children. These men were dragged back and hurled sprawling across the deck. Six of them, screaming with fear, struggled to their feet and made a second attempt to rush to the boats.

About ten shots sounded in quick succession. The six cowardly men were stopped in their tracks, staggered and collapsed one after another. At least two of them vainly attempted to creep toward the boats again. The others lay quite still. This scene of bloodshed served its purpose. In that particular section of the deck there was no further attempt to violate the rule of "women and children first."

"I helped fill the boats with women," said Thomas Whiteley, who was a waiter on the Titanic. "Collapsible boat No. 2 on the starboard jammed. The second officer was hacking at the ropes with a knife and I was being dragged around the deck by that rope when I looked up and saw the boat, with all aboard, turn turtle. In some way I got overboard myself and clung to an oak dresser. I wasn't more than sixty feet from the Titanic when she went down. Her big stern rose up in the air and she went down bow first. I saw all the machinery drop out of her.

HENRY B. HARRIS

Henry B. Harris, of New York, a theatrical manager, was one of the men who showed superb courage in the crisis. When the life-boats were first being filled, and before there was any panic, Mr. Harris went to the side of his wife before the boat was lowered away.

"Women first," shouted one of the ship's officers. Mr. Harris glanced up and saw that the remark was addressed to him.

"All right," he replied coolly. "Good-bye, my dear," he said, as he kissed his wife, pressed her a moment to his breast, and then climbed back to the Titanic's deck.

THREE EXPLOSIONS

Up to this time there had been no panic; but about one hour before the ship plunged to the bottom there were three separate explosions of bulkheads as the vessel filled. These were at intervals of about fifteen minutes. From that time there was a different scene. The rush for the remaining boats became a stampede.

The stokers rushed up from below and tried to beat a path through the steerage men and women and through the sailors and officers, to get into the boats. They had their iron bars and shovels, and they struck down all who stood in their way.

The first to come up from the depths of the ship was an engineer. From what he is reported to have said it is probable that the steam fittings were broken and many were scalded to death when the Titanic lifted. He said he had to dash through a narrow place beside a broken pipe and his back was frightfully scalded.

Right at his heels came the stokers. The officers had pistols, but they could not use them at first for fear of killing the women and children. The sailors fought with their fists and many of them took the stoke bars and shovels from the stokers and used them to beat back the others.

Many of the coal-passers and stokers who had been driven back from the boats went to the rail, and whenever a boat was filled and lowered several of them jumped overboard and swam toward it trying to climb aboard. Several of the survivors said that men who swam to the sides of their boats were pulled in or climbed in.

Dozens of the cabin passengers were witnesses of some of the frightful scenes on the steerage deck. The steerage survivors said that ten women from the upper decks were the only cool passengers in the life-boat, and they tried to quiet the steerage women, who were nearly all crazed with fear and grief.

OTHER HEROES

Among the chivalrous young heroes of the Titanic disaster were Washington A. Roebling, 2d, and Howard Case, London representative of the Vacuum Oil Company. Both were urged repeatedly to take places in life-boats, but scorned the opportunity, while working against time to save the women aboard the ill-fated ship. They went to their death, it is said by survivors, with smiles on their faces.

Both of these young men aided in the saving of Mrs. William T. Graham, wife of the president of the American Can Company, and Mrs. Graham's nineteen-year-old daughter, Margaret.

Afterwards relating some of her experiences Mrs. Graham said:

"There was a rap at the door. It was a passenger whom we had met shortly after the ship left Liverpool, and his name was Roebling—Washington A. Roebling, 2d. He was a gentleman and a brave man. He warned us of the danger and told us that it would be best to be prepared for an emergency. We heeded his warning, and I looked out of my window and saw a great big iceberg facing us. Immediately I knew what had happened and we lost no time after that to get out into the saloon.

"In one of the gangways I met an officer of the ship.

" 'What is the matter?' I asked him.

" 'We've only burst two pipes,' he said, 'Everything is all right, don't worry.'

" 'But what makes the ship list so?' I asked.

" 'Oh, that's nothing,' he replied, and walked away.

"Mr. Case advised us to get into a boat.

" 'And what are you going to do?' we asked him.

" 'Oh,' he replied, 'I'll take a chance and stay here.'

"Just at that time they were filling up the third life-boat on the port side of the ship. I thought at the time that it was the third boat which had been lowered, but I found out later that they had lowered other boats on the other side, where the people were more excited because they were sinking on that side.

"Just then Mr. Roebling came up too and told us to hurry and get into the third boat. Mr. Roebling and Mr. Case bustled our party of three into that boat in less time than it takes to tell it. They were both working hard to help the women and children. The boat was fairly crowded when we three were pushed into it, and a few men jumped in at the last moment, but Mr. Roebling and Mr. Case stood at the rail and made no attempt to get into the boat.

"They shouted good-bye to us. What do you think Mr. Case did then? He just calmly lighted a cigarette and waved us good-bye with his hand. Mr. Roebling stood there, too—I can see him now. I am sure that he knew that the ship would go to the bottom. But both just stood there."

IN THE FACE OF DEATH

Scenes on the sinking vessel grew more tragic as the remaining passengers faced the awful certainty that death must be the portion of the majority, death in the darkness of a wintry sea studded with its ice monuments like the marble shafts in some vast cemetery.

In that hour, when cherished illusions of possible safety had all but vanished, manhood and womanhood aboard the Titanic rose to their sublimest heights. It was in that crisis of the direst extremity that many brave women deliberately rejected life and chose rather to remain and die with the men whom they loved.

DEATH FAILS TO PART MR. AND MRS. STRAUS

"I will not leave my husband," said Mrs. Isidor Straus. "We are old; we can best die together," and she turned from those who would have forced her into one of the boats and clung to the man who had been the partner of her joys and sorrows. Thus they stood hand in hand and heart to heart, comforting each other until the sea claimed them, united in death as they had been through a long life.

"Greater love hath no man than this, that a man lay down his life for his friends."

Miss Elizabeth Evans fulfilled this final test of affection laid down by the Divine Master. The girl was the niece of the wife of Magistrate Cornell, of New York. She was placed in the same boat with many other women. As it was about to be lowered away it was found that the craft contained one more than its full quota of passengers.

The grim question arose as to which of them should surrender her place and her chance of safety. Beside Miss Evans sat Mrs. J. J. Brown, of Denver, the mother of several children. Miss Evans was the first to volunteer to yield to another.

GIRL STEPS BACK TO DOOM

"Your need is greater than mine," said she to Mrs. Brown. "You have children who need you, and I have none."

So saying she arose from the boat and stepped back upon the deck. The girl found no later refuge and was one of those who went down with the ship. She was twenty-five years old and was beloved by all who knew her.

Mrs. Brown thereafter showed the spirit which had made her also volunteer to leave the boat. There were only three men in the boat and but one of them rowed. Mrs. Brown, who was raised on the water, immediately picked up one of the heavy sweeps and began to pull.

In the boat which carried Mrs. Cornell and Mrs. Appleton there were places for seventeen more than were carried. This too was undermanned and the two women at once took their places at the oars.

The Countess of Rothes was pulling at the oars of her boat, likewise undermanned because the crew preferred to stay behind.

Miss Bentham, of Rochester, showed splendid courage. She happened to be in a life-boat which was very much crowded—so much so that one sailor had to sit with his feet dangling in the icy cold water, and as time went on the sufferings of the man from the cold were apparent. Miss Bentham arose from her place and had the man turn around while she took her place with her feet in the water.

Scarcely any of the life-boats were properly manned. Two, filled with women and children, capsized immediately, while the collapsible boats were only temporarily useful They soon filled with

THE ETERNAL COLLISION

water. In one boat eighteen or twenty persons sat in water above their knees for six hours.

Eight men in this boat were overcome, died and were thrown overboard. Two women were in this boat, and one succumbed after a few hours and one was saved.

The accident was reported as entirely the result of carelessness and lack of necessary equipment. There were boats for only one third of the passengers, there were no search lights; the lifeboats were not supplied with food or safety appliances; there were no lanterns on the life-boats; there was no way to raise sails, as there was no one who understood managing a sailboat.

Mrs. Hogeboom explained that the new equipment of masts and sails in the boats was carefully wrapped and bound with twine. The men undertook to unfasten them, but found it necessary to cut the ropes. They had no knives, and in their frenzy they went about asking the ill-clad women if they had knives. The sails were never hoisted.

THE MONEY BOAT

Thomas Whiteley, a first saloon steward, in telling of various experiences of the disaster that had come to his knowledge, said that on one of the first boats lowered the only passengers aboard were a man whom he was told was an American millionaire, his wife, child and two valets. The others in the boat were firemen and coal trimmers, he said, seven in number, whom the man had promised to pay well if they would man the life-boat. They made only thirteen in all.

"I do not know the man's name," said Whiteley. "I heard it, but have forgotten it. But I saw an order for five pounds which this man gave to each of the crew of his boat after they got aboard the Carpathia. It was on a piece of ordinary paper addressed to the Coutts Bank of England.

"We called that boat the 'money boat.' It was lowered from the starboard side and was one of the first off. Our orders were to load the life-boats beginning forward on the port side, working

IN THE DRIFTING LIFE-BOATS

Here the intense physical suffering from cold and exposure, added to the mental agony preceding and accompanying it, overwhelmed many of the boats' occupants. In consequence, the Carpathia, which rescued the survivors, was literally a floating hospital during her sad journey back to New York.

LIFE-BOATS, AS SEEN FROM THE CARPATHIA

Photographs taken from the rescue ship as she reached the first boats carrying the Titanic's sufferers.

aft and then back on the starboard. This man paid the firemen to lower a starboard boat before the officers had given the order."

Whiteley's own experience was a hard one. When the uncoiling rope, which entangled his feet, threw him into the sea, it furrowed the flesh of his leg, but he did not feel the pain until he was safe aboard the Carpathia.

"I floated on my life-preserver for several hours," he said, "then I came across a big oak dresser with two men clinging to it. I hung on to this till daybreak and the two men dropped off. When the sun came up I saw the collapsible raft in the distance, just black with men. They were all standing up, and I swam to it—almost a mile, it seemed to me—and they would not let me aboard. Mr. Lightoller, the second officer, was one of them.

" 'It's thirty-one lives against yours,' he said, 'you can't come aboard. There's not room.'

"I pleaded with him in vain, and then I confess I prayed that somebody might die, so I could take his place. It was only human. And then some one did die, and they let me aboard.

"By and by, we saw seven life-boats lashed together, and we were taken into them."

MEN SHOT DOWN

The officers had to assert their authority by force, and three foreigners from the steerage who tried to force their way in among the women and children were shot down without mercy.

Robert Daniel, a Philadelphia passenger, told of terrible scenes at this period of the disaster. He said men fought and bit and struck one another like madmen, and exhibited wounds upon his face to prove the assertion. Mr. Daniel said that he was picked up naked from the ice-cold water and almost perished from exposure before he was rescued. He and others told how the Titanic's bow was completely torn away by the impact with the berg.

K. Whiteman, of Palmyra, N. J., the Titanic's barber, was lowering boats on deck after the collision, and declared the officers on the bridge, one of them First Officer Murdock, promptly worked the electrical apparatus for closing the watertight compartments. He believed the machinery was in some way so damaged by the crash that the front compartments failed to close tightly, although the rear ones were secure.

Whiteman's manner of escape was unique. He was blown off the deck by the second of the two explosions of the boilers, and was in the water more than two hours before he was picked up by a raft.

"The explosions," Whiteman said, "were caused by the rushing in of the icy water on the boilers. A bundle of deck chairs, roped together, was blown off the deck with me, and I struck my back, injuring my spine, but it served as a temporary raft.

"The crew and passengers had faith in the bulkhead system to save the ship and we were lowering a collapsible boat, all confident the ship would get through, when she took a terrific dip forward and the water swept over the deck and into the engine rooms.

"The bow went clean down, and I caught the pile of chairs as I was washed up against the rim. Then came the explosions which blew me fifteen feet.

"After the water had filled the forward compartments, the ones at the stern could not save her, although they did delay the ship's going down. If it wasn't for the compartments hardly anyone could have got away.

A SAD MESSAGE

One of the Titanic's stewards, Johnson by name, carried this message to the sorrowing widow of Benjamin Guggenheim:

"When Mr. Guggenheim realized that there was grave danger," said the room steward, "he advised his secretary, who also died, to dress fully and he himself did the same. Mr. Guggenheim, who was cool and collected as he was pulling on his outer garments, said to the steward:—

PREPARED TO DIE BRAVELY

" 'I think there is grave doubt that the men will get off safely. I am willing to remain and play the man's game, if there are not enough boats for more than the women and children. I won't die here like a beast. I'll meet my end as a man.'

"There was a pause and then Mr. Guggenheim continued.

" 'Tell my wife, Johnson, if it should happen that my secretary and I both go down and you are saved, tell her I played the game out straight and to the end. No woman shall be left aboard this ship because Ben Guggenheim was a coward.

" 'Tell her that my last thoughts will be of her and of our girls, but that my duty now is to these unfortunate women and children on this ship. Tell her I will meet whatever fate is in store for me, knowing she will approve of what I do.' "

In telling the story the room steward said the last he saw of Mr. Guggenheim was when he stood fully dressed upon the upper deck talking calmly with Colonel Astor and Major Butt.

Before the last of the boats got away, according to some of the passengers' narratives, there were more than fifty shots fired upon the decks by officers or others in the effort to maintain the discipline that until then had been well preserved.

THE SINKING VESSEL

Richard Norris Williams, Jr., one of the survivors of the Titanic, saw his father killed by being crushed by one of the tremendous funnels of the sinking vessel.

"We stood on deck watching the life-boats of the Titanic being filled and lowered into the water," said Mr. Williams. "The water was nearly up to our waists and the ship was about at her last. Suddenly one of the great funnels fell. I sprang aside, endeavoring to pull Father with me. A moment later the funnel was swept overboard and the body of Father went with it.

"I sprang overboard and swam through the ice to a life-raft, and was pulled aboard. There were five men and one woman on the raft. Occasionally we were swept off into the sea, but always managed to crawl back.

"A sailor lighted a cigarette and flung the match carelessly among the women. Several screamed, fearing they would be set on fire. The sailor replied: 'We are going to hell anyway and we might as well be cremated now as then.'"

A huge cake of ice was the means of aiding Emile Portaleppi, of Italy, in his hairbreadth escape from death when the Titanic went down. Portaleppi, a second class passenger, was awakened by the explosion of one of the bulkheads of the ship. He hurried to the deck, strapped a life-preserver around him and leaped into the sea. With the aid of the preserver and by holding to a cake of ice he managed to keep afloat until one of the life-boats picked him up. There were thirty-five other people in the boat, he said, when he was hauled aboard.

THE COWARD

Somewhere in the shadow of the appalling Titanic disaster slinks—still living by the inexplicable grace of God—a cur in human shape, today the most despicable human being in world.

In that grim midnight hour, already great in history, he found himself hemmed in by the band of heroes whose watchword and countersign rang out across the deep—"Women and children first!"

What did he do? He scuttled to the stateroom deck, put on a woman's skirt, a woman's hat and a woman's veil, and picking his crafty way back among the brave and chivalric men who guarded the rail of the doomed ship, he filched a seat in one of the life-boats and saved his skin.

His name is on that list of branded rescued men who were neither picked up from the sea when the ship went down nor were in the boats under orders to help get them safe away. His identity is not yet known, though it will be in good time. So foul an act as that will out like murder.

The eyes of strong men who have read this crowded record of golden deeds, who have read and re-read that deathless roll of honor of the dead, are still wet with tears of pity and of pride. This man still lives. Surely he was born and saved to set for men a new standard by which to measure infamy and shame.

It is well that there was sufficient heroism on board the Titanic to neutralize the horrors of the cowardice. When the first order was given for the men to stand back, there were a dozen or more who pushed forward and said that men would be needed to row the life-boats and that they would volunteer for the work.

The officers tried to pick out the ones that volunteered merely for service and to eliminate those who volunteered merely to save their own lives. This elimination process, however, was not wholly successful.

THE DOOMED MEN

As the ship began to settle to starboard, heeling at an angle of nearly forty-five degrees, those who had believed it was all right to stick by the ship began to have doubts, and a few jumped into the sea. They were followed immediately by others, and in a few minutes there were scores swimming around. Nearly all of them wore life-preservers. One man, who had a Pomeranian dog, leaped overboard with it and striking a piece of wreckage was badly stunned. He recovered after a few minutes and swam toward one of the life-boats and was taken aboard.

Said one survivor, speaking of the men who remained on the ship: "There they stood—Major Butt, Colonel Astor waving a farewell to his wife, Mr. Thayer, Mr. Case, Mr. Clarence Moore, Mr. Widener, all multimillionaires, and hundreds of other men, bravely smiling at us all. Never have I seen such chivalry and fortitude. Such courage in the face of fate horrible to contemplate filled us even then with wonder and admiration."

Why were men saved? ask others who seek to make the occasional male survivor a hissing scorn; and yet the testimony makes it clear that for a long time during that ordeal the more frightful position seemed to many to be in the frail boats in the vast relentless sea, and that some men had to be tumbled into the boats under orders from the officers. Others express the deepest indignation that 210 sailors were rescued; the testimony shows that most of these sailors were in the welter of ice and water into which they had been thrown from the ship's deck when she sank; they were human beings and so were picked up and saved.

"WOMEN AND CHILDREN FIRST"

The one alleviating circumstance in the otherwise immitigable tragedy is the fact that so many of the men stood aside really with out the necessity for the order, "Women and children first," and insisted that the weaker sex should first have places in the boats.

There were men whose word of command swayed boards of directors, governed institutions, disposed of millions. They were accustomed merely to pronounce a wish to have it gratified. Thousands "posted at their bidding"; the complexion, of the market altered hue when they nodded; they bought what they wanted, and for one of the humblest fishing smacks or a dory they could have given the price that was paid to build and launch the ship that has become the most imposing mausoleum that ever housed the bones of men since the Pyramids rose from the desert sands.

But these men stood aside—one can see them!—and gave place not merely to the delicate and the refined, but to the scared Czech woman from the steerage, with her baby at her breast; the Croatian with a toddler by her side, coming through the very gate of Death to the imagined Eden of America.

To many of those who went it was harder to go than to stay there on the vessel gaping with its mortal wounds and ready to go down. It meant that tossing on the waters they must wait in suspense, hour after hour even after the lights of the ship were engulfed in appalling darkness, hoping against hope for the miracle of a rescue dearer to them than their own lives.

CHAPTER VII

Left to Their Fate

COOLNESS AND HEROISM OF THOSE LEFT TO PERISH—SUICIDE
OF MURDOCK—CAPTAIN SMITH'S END—THE SHIP'S BAND PLAYS A
NOBLE HYMN AS THE VESSEL GOES DOWN.

THE general feeling aboard the ship after the boats had left her sides was that she would not survive her wound, but the passengers who remained aboard displayed the utmost heroism.

William T. Stead, the famous English journalist, was so little alarmed that he calmly discussed with one of the passengers the probable height of the iceberg after the Titanic had shot into it.

Confidence in the ability of the Titanic to remain afloat doubtlessly led many of the passengers to death. The theory that the great ship was unsinkable remained with hundreds who had entrusted themselves to the gigantic hulk, long after the officers knew that the vessel could not survive.

The captain and officers behaved with superb gallantry, and there was perfect order and discipline among those who were aboard, even after all hope had been abandoned for the salvation of the ship.

Many women went down, steerage women who were unable to get to the upper decks where the boats were launched, maids who were overlooked in the confusion, cabin passengers who refused to desert their husbands or who reached the decks after the last of the life-boats was gone and the ship was settling for her final plunge to the bottom of the Atlantic.

Narratives of survivors do not bear out the supposition that the final hours upon the vessel's decks were passed in darkness. They say the electric lighting plant held out until the last, and that even as they watched the ship sink, from their places in the floating life-boats, her lights were gleaming in long rows as she plunged under by the head. Just before she sank, some of the refugees say, the ship broke in two abaft the engine room after the bulkhead explosions had occurred.

COLONEL ASTOR'S DEATH

To Colonel Astor's death Philip Mock bears this testimony:

"Many men were hanging on to rafts in the sea. William T. Stead and Colonel Astor were among them. Their feet and hands froze and they had to let go. Both were drowned."

The last man among the survivors to speak to Colonel Astor was K. Whiteman, the ship's barber.

"I shaved Colonel Astor Sunday afternoon," said Whiteman. He was a pleasant, affable man, and that awful night when I found myself standing beside him on the passenger deck, helping to put the women into the boats, I spoke to him.

"Where is your life-belt?" I asked him.

" 'I didn't think there would be any need of it,' he said.

" 'Get one while there is time,' I told him. 'The last boat is gone, and we are done for.'

" 'No,' he said, 'I think there are some life-boats to be launched, and we may get on one of them.'

" 'There are no life-rafts,' I told him, 'and the ship is going to sink. I am going to jump overboard and take a chance on swimming out and being picked up by one of the boats. Better come along.'

" 'No, thank you,' he said, calmly, 'I think I'll have to stick.'

"I asked him if he would mind shaking hands with me. He said, 'With pleasure,' gave me a hearty grip, and then I climbed up on the rail and jumped overboard. I was in the water nearly four hours before one of the boats picked me up."

CAPTAIN WASHED OVERBOARD

Murdock's last orders were to Quartermaster Moody and a few other petty officers who had taken their places in the rigid discipline of the ship and were lowering the boats. Captain Smith came up to him on the bridge several times and then rushed down again. They spoke to one another only in monosyllables.

There were stories that Captain Smith, when he saw the ship actually going down, had committed suicide. There is no basis for such tales. The captain, according to the testimony of those who were near him almost until the last, was admirably cool. He carried a revolver in his hand, ready to use it on anyone who disobeyed orders.

"I want every man to act like a man for manhood's sake," he said, "and if they don't, a bullet awaits the coward."

With the revolver in his hand—a fact that undoubtedly gave rise to the suicide theory—the captain moved up and down the deck. He gave the order for each life-boat to make off and he remained until every boat was gone. Standing on the bridge he finally called out the order: "Each man save himself." At that moment all discipline fled. It was the last call of death. If there had been any hope among those on board before, the hope now had fled.

The bearded admiral of the White Star Line fleet, with every life-saving device launched from the decks, was returning to the deck to perform the sacred office of going down with his ship when a wave dashed over the side and tore him from the ladder.

The Titanic was sinking rapidly by the head, with the twisting sidelong motion that was soon to aim her on her course two miles down. Murdock saw the skipper swept out, but did not move. Captain Smith was but one of a multitude of lost at that moment. Murdock may have known that the last desperate thought of the gray mariner was to get upon his bridge and die in command. That the old man could not have done this may have had something to do with Murdock's suicidal inspiration. Of that no man may say or safely guess.

The wave that swept the skipper out bore him almost to the thwart of a crowded life-boat. Hands reached out, but he wrenched himself away, turned and swam back toward the ship.

Some say that he said, "Good-bye, I'm going back to the ship."

He disappeared for a moment, then reappeared where a rail was slipping under water. Cool and courageous to the end, loyal to his duty under the most difficult circumstances, he showed himself a noble captain, and he died a noble death.

SAW BOTH OFFICERS PERISH

Quartermaster Moody saw all this, watched the skipper scramble aboard again onto the submerged decks, and then vanish altogether in a great billow.

As Moody's eye lost sight of the skipper in this confusion of waters it again shifted to the bridge, and just in time to see Murdock take his life. The man's face was turned toward him, Moody said, and he could not mistake it. There were still many gleaming lights on the ship, flickering out like little groups of vanishing stars, and with the clear starshine on the waters there was nothing to cloud or break the quarter master's vision.

"I saw Murdock die by his own hand," said Moody, "saw the flash from his gun, heard the crack that followed the flash and then saw him plunge over on his face."

Others report hearing several pistol shots on the decks below the bridge, but amid the groans and shrieks and cries, shouted orders and all that vast orchestra of sounds that broke upon the air they must have been faint periods of punctuation.

BAND PLAYED ITS OWN DIRGE

The band had broken out in the strains of "Nearer, My God, to Thee," some minutes before Murdock lifted the revolver to his head, fired and toppled over on his face. Moody saw all this in a vision that filled his brain, while his ears drank in the tragic strain of the beautiful hymn that the band played as their own dirge, even to the moment when the waters sucked them down.

Wherever Murdock's eye swept the water in that instant, before he drew his revolver, it looked upon veritable seas of drowning men and women. From the decks there came to him the shrieks and groans of the caged and drowning, for whom all hope of escape was utterly vanished. He evidently never gave a

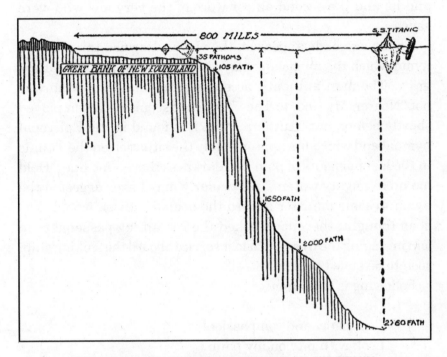

THE NATURE OF THE INJURY SUSTAINED BY THE TITANIC

thought to the possibility of saving himself, his mind freezing with the horrors he beheld and having room for just one central idea—swift extinction.

The strains of the hymn and the frantic cries of the dying blended in a symphony of sorrow.

Led by the green light, under the light of stars, the boats drew away, and the bow, then the quarter, then the stacks and last the stern of the marvel ship of a few days before passed beneath the waters. The great force of the ship's sinking was unaided by any violence of the elements, and the suction, not so great as had been feared, rocked but mildly the group of boats now a quarter of a mile distant from it.

Just before the Titanic disappeared from view men and women leaped from the stern. More than a hundred men, according to Colonel Gracie, jumped at the last. Gracie was among the number and he and the second officer were of the very few who were saved.

As the vessel disappeared, the waves drowned the majestic hymn which the musicians played as they went to their watery grave. The most authentic accounts agree that this hymn was not "Nearer, My God, to Thee," which it seems had been played shortly before, but "Autumn," which is found in the Episcopal hymnal and which fits appropriately the situation on the Titanic in the last moments of pain and darkness there. One line, "Hold me up in mighty waters," particularly may have suggested the hymn to some minister aboard the doomed vessel, who, it has been thought, thereupon asked the remaining passengers to join in singing the hymn, in a last service aboard the sinking ship, soon to be ended by death itself.

Following is the hymn:

> God of mercy and compassion!
>   Look with pity on my pain:
> Hear a mournful, broken spirit
>   Prostrate at Thy feet complain:
> Many are my foes, and mighty;
>   Strength to conquer I have none;
> Nothing can uphold my goings
>   But Thy blessed Self alone.
>
> Saviour, look on Thy beloved;
>   Triumph over all my foes;
> Turn to heavenly joy my mourning,
>   Turn to gladness all my woes;

CARPATHIA
The Cunard liner which brought the survivors of the Titanic to New York.

Copyright by Underwood & Underwood, N. Y.

THE HERO WIRELESS OPERATOR OF THE TITANIC

Photograph of Harold Bride, one of the two wireless operators on board the Titanic, being carried ashore from the Steamship Carpathia by two ship's officers. Bride, one of the last men to leave the ship, jumped into the sea and floated around in the water until rescued. When taken into a life-boat his feet were badly frost-bitten and became wedged into the slats at the bottom of the life-boat and were wrenched severely. Although suffering great pain, he helped the wireless operator of the Carpathia, Harold Thomas Catton, to send hundreds of wireless messages ashore.

Live or die, or work or suffer,
    Let my weary soul abide,
In all changes whatsoever
    Sure and steadfast by Thy side.

When temptations fierce assault me,
    When my enemies I find,
Sin and guilt, and death and Satan,
    All against my soul combined,
Hold me up in mighty waters,
    Keep my eyes on things above,
Righteousness, divine Atonement,
    Peace, and everlasting Love.

It was a little lame schoolmaster, Tyrtaeus, who aroused the Spartans by his poetry and led them to victory against the foe.

It was the musicians of the band of the Titanic—poor men, paid a few dollars a week—who played the music to keep up the courage of the souls aboard the sinking ship.

"The way the band kept playing was a noble thing," says the wireless operator. "I heard it first while we were working the wireless, when there was a rag-time tune for us, and the last I saw of the band, when I was floating, struggling in the icy water, it was still on deck, playing 'Autumn.' How those brave fellows ever did it I cannot imagine."

Perhaps that music, made in the face of death, would not have satisfied the exacting critical sense. It may be that the chilled fingers faltered on the pistons of the cornet or at the valves of the French horn, that the time was irregular and that by an organ in a church, with a decorous congregation, the hymns they chose would have been better played and sung. But surely that music went up to God from the souls of drowning men, and was not less acceptable than the song of songs no mortal ear may hear, the harps of the seraphs and the choiring cherubim. Under the sea the music-makers lie, still in their fingers clutching the broken and battered means of melody; but over the strident voice of warring winds and the sound of many waters there rises their chant eternally; and though the musicians lie hushed and cold at the sea's heart, their music is heard forevermore.

LAST MOMENTS

That great ship, which started out as proudly, went down to her death like some grim, silent juggernaut, drunk with carnage and anxious to stop the throbbing of her own heart at the bottom of the sea. Charles H. Lightoller, second officer of the Titanic, tells the story this way:

"I stuck to the ship until the water came up to my ankles. There had been no lamentations, no demonstrations either from the men passengers as they saw the last life-boat go, and there was no wailing or crying, no outburst from the men who lined the ship's rail as the Titanic disappeared from sight.

"The men stood quietly as if they were in church. They knew that they were in the sight of God; that in a moment judgment would be passed upon them. Finally, the ship took a dive, reeling for a moment, then plunging. I was sucked to the side of the ship against the grating over the blower for the exhaust. There was an explosion. It blew me to the surface again, only to be sucked back again by the water rushing into the ship.

"This time I landed against the grating over the pipes, which furnish a draught for the funnels, and stuck there. There was another explosion, and I came to the surface. The ship seemed to be heaving tremendous sighs as she went down. I found myself not many feet from the ship, but on the other side of it. The ship had turned around while I was under the water.

"I came up near a collapsible life-boat and grabbed it. Many men were in the water near me. They had jumped at the last minute. A funnel fell within four inches of me and killed one of the swimmers. Thirty clung to the capsized boat, and a life-boat, with forty survivors in it already, finally took them off.

"George D. Widener and Harry Elkins Widener were among

those who jumped at the last minute. So did Robert Williams Daniel. The three of them went down together. Daniel struck out, lashing the water with his arms until he had made a point far distant from the sinking monster of the sea. Later he was picked up by one of the passing life-boats.

"The Wideners were not seen again, nor was John Bo Thayer, who went down on the boat. 'Jack' Thayer, who was literally thrown off the Titanic by an explosion, after he had refused to leave the men to go with his mother, floated around on a raft for an hour before he was picked up."

AFLOAT WITH JACK THAYER

Graphic accounts of the final plunge of the Titanic were related by two Englishmen, survivors by the merest chance. One of them struggled for hours to hold himself afloat on an overturned collapsible life-boat, to one end of which John B. Thayer, Jr., of Philadelphia, whose father perished, hung until rescued.

The men gave their names as A. H. Barkworth, justice of the peace of East Riding, Yorkshire, England, and W. J. Mellers, of Christ Church Terrace, Chelsea, London. The latter, a young man, had started for this country with his savings to seek his fortune, and lost all but his life.

Mellers, like Quartermaster Moody, said Captain Smith did not commit suicide. The captain jumped from the bridge, Mellers declares, and he heard him say to his officers and crew: "You have done your duty, boys. Now every man for himself." Mellers and Barkworth, who say their names have been spelled incorrectly in most of the lists of survivors, both declare there were three distinct explosions before the Titanic broke in two, and bow section first, and stern part last, settled with her human cargo into the sea.

Her four whistles kept up a deafening blast until the explosions, declare the men. The death cries from the shrill throats of the blatant steam screechers beside the smokestacks so rent the air that conversation among the passengers was possible only when one yelled into the ear of a fellow-unfortunate.

"I did not know the Thayer family well," declared Mr. Barkworth, "but I had met young Thayer, a clean-cut chap, and his father on the trip. The lad and I struggled in the water for several hours endeavoring to hold afloat by grabbing to the sides and end of an overturned life-boat. Now and again we lost our grip and fell back into the water. I did not recognize young Thayer in the darkness, as we struggled for our lives, but I did recall having met him before when we were picked up by a life-boat. We were saved by the merest chance, because the survivors on a life-boat that rescued us hesitated in doing so, it seemed, fearing perhaps that additional burdens would swamp the frail craft.

"I considered my fur overcoat helped to keep me afloat. I had a life preserver over it, under my arms, but it would not have held me up so well out of the water but for the coat. The fur of the coat seemed not to get wet through, and retained a certain amount of air that added to buoyancy. I shall never part with it.

"The testimony of J. Bruce Ismay, managing director of the White Star Line, that he had not heard explosions before the Titanic settled, indicates that he must have gotten some distance from her in his life-boat. There were three distinct explosions and the ship broke in the center. The bow settled headlong first, and the stern last. I was looking toward her from the raft to which young Thayer and I had clung."

HOW CAPTAIN SMITH DIED

Barkworth jumped, just before the Titanic went down. He said there were enough life-preservers for all the passengers, but in the confusion many may not have known where to look for them. Mellers, who had donned a life-preserver, was hurled into the air, from the bow of the ship by the force of the explosion, which he believed caused the Titanic to part in the center.

"I was not far from where Captain Smith stood on the ridge, giving full orders to his men," said Mellers. "The brave old seaman was crying, but he had stuck heroically to the last. He did not shoot himself. He jumped from the bridge when he had done all he could. I heard his final instructions to his crew, and recall that his last words were: 'You have done your duty, boys. Now every man for himself.'

"I thought I was doomed to go down with the rest. I stood on the deck, awaiting my fate, fearing to jump from the ship. Then came a grinding noise, followed by two others, and I was hurled into the deep. Great waves engulfed me, but I was not drawn toward the ship, so that I believe there was little suction. I swam about for more than one hour before I was picked up by a boat."

A FAITHFUL OFFICER

Charles Herbert Lightoller, previously mentioned, stood by the ship until the last, working to get the passengers away, and when it appeared that he had made his last trip he went up high on the officers' quarters and made the best dive he knew how to make just as the ship plunged down to the depths. This is an excerpt from his testimony before the Senate investigating committee:

"What time did you leave the ship?"

"I didn't leave it."

"Did it leave you?"

"Yes, Sir."

Children shall hear that episode sung in after years and his own descendants shall recite it to their bairns. Mr. Lightolier acted as an officer and gentleman should, and he was not the only one.

A MESSAGE FROM A NOTORIOUS GAMBLER

That Jay Yates, gambler, confidence man and fugitive from justice, known to the police and in sporting circles as J. H. Rogers, went down with the Titanic after assisting many women aboard life-boats, became known when a note, written on a blank page torn from a diary, was delivered to his sister. There is a facsimile of the note on the next page.

This note was given by Rogers to a woman he was helping into a life-boat. The woman, who signed herself "Survivor," inclosed the note with the following letter:

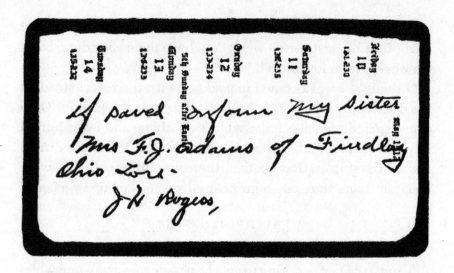

"You will find note that was handed to me as I was leaving the Titanic. Am stranger to this man, but think he was a card player. He helped me aboard a life-boat and I saw him help others. Before we were lowered I saw him jump into the sea. If picked up I did not recognize him on the Carpathia. I don't think he was registered on the ship under his right name."

Rogers' mother, Mrs. Mary A. Yates, an old woman, broke down when she learned her son had perished.

"Thank God I know where he is now," she sobbed. "I have not heard from him for two years. The last news I had from him he was in London."

FIFTY LADS MET DEATH

Among the many hundreds of heroic souls who went bravely and quietly to their end were fifty happy-go-lucky youngsters shipped as bell boys or messengers to serve the first cabin passengers. James Humphreys, a quartermaster, who commanded life-boat No. 11, told a little story that shows how these fifty lads met death.

Humphreys said the boys were called to their regular posts in the main cabin entry and taken in charge by their captain, a steward. They were ordered to remain in the cabin and not get in the way. Throughout the first hour of confusion and terror these lads sat quietly on their benches in various parts of the first cabin.

Then, just toward the end when the order was passed around that the ship was going down and every man was free to save himself, if he kept away from the life-boats in which the women were being taken, the bell boys scattered to all parts of the ship.

Humphreys said he saw numbers of them smoking cigarettes and joking with the passengers. They seemed to think that their violation of the rule against smoking while on duty was a sufficient breach of discipline.

Not one of them attempted to enter a life-boat. Not one of them was saved.

THE HEROES WHO REMAINED

The women who left the ship, the men who remained—there is little to choose between them for heroism. Many of the women compelled to take to the boats would have stayed, had it been possible, to share the fate of their nearest and dearest, without whom their lives are crippled, broken and disconsolate.

The heroes who remained would have said, with Grenville: "We have only done our duty, as a man is bound to do." They sought no palms or crowns of martyrdom. "They also serve who only stand and wait," and their first action was merely to step aside and give places in the boats to women and children, some of whom were too young to comprehend or to remember.

There was no debate as to whether the life of a financier, a master of business, was rated higher in the scale of values than that of an ignorant peasant mother. A woman was a woman, whether she wore rags or pearls. A life was given for a life, with no assertion that one was priceless and the other comparatively valueless.

Many of those who elected to remain might have escaped. "Chivalry" is a mild appellation for their conduct. Some of the vaunted knights of old were desperate cowards by comparison.

A fight in the open field, or jousting in the tournament, did not call out the manhood in a man as did the waiting till the great ship took the final plunge, in the knowledge that the seas round about were covered with loving and yearning witnesses whose own salvation was not assured.

When the roll is called hereafter of those who are "purged of pride because they died, who know the worth of their days," let the names of the men who went down with the Titanic be found written there in the sight of God and men.

THE OBVIOUS LESSON

And, whatever view of the accident be taken, whether the moralist shall use it to point the text of a solemn or denunciatory warning, or whether the materialist, swinging to the other extreme, scouts any other theory than that of the "fortuitous concurrence of atoms," there is scarcely a thinking mortal who has heard of what happened who has not been deeply stirred, in the sense of a personal bereavement, to a profound humility and the conviction of his own insignificance in the greater universal scheme.

Many there are whom the influences of religion do not move, and upon whose hearts most generous sentiments knock in vain, who still are overawed and bowed by the magnitude of this catastrophe. No matter what they believe about it, the effect is the same. The effect is to reduce a man from the swaggering braggart—the vainglorious lord of what he sees—the self-made master of fate, of nature, of time, of space, of everything—to his true microscopic stature in the cosmos. He goes in tears to put together again the fragments of the few, small, pitiful things that belonged to him.

> "Though Love may pine, and Reason chafe,
> There came a Voice without reply."

The only comfort, all that can bring surcease of sorrow, is that men fashioned in the image of their Maker rose to the emergency like heroes, and went to their grave as bravely as any who have given their lives at any time in war. The hearts of those who waited on the land, and agonized, and were impotent to save, have been laid upon the same altars of sacrifice. The mourning of those who will not be comforted rises from alien lands together with our own in a common broken intercession. How little is the 882 feet of the "monster" that we launched compared with the arc of the rainbow we can see even in our grief spanning the frozen boreal mist!

"The best of what we do and are,
Just God, forgive!"

THE ANCIENT SACRIFICE

And still our work must go on. It is the business of men and women neither to give way to unavailing grief nor to yield to the crushing incubus of despair, but to find hope that is at the bottom of everything, even at the bottom of the sea where that glorious virgin of the ocean is lying.

"And when she took unto herself a mate
She must espouse the everlasting sea."

Even so, for any progress of the race, there must be the ancient sacrifice of man's own stubborn heart, and all his pride. He must forever "lay in dust life's glory dead." He cannot rise to the height it was intended he should reach till he has plumbed the depths, till he has devoured the bread of the bitterest affliction, till he has known the ache of hopes deferred, of anxious expectation disappointed, of dreams that are not to be fulfilled this side of the river that waters the meads of Paradise. There still must be a reason why it is not an unhappy thing to be taken from "the world we know to one a wonder still," and so that we go bravely, what does it matter, the mode of our going? It was not only those who stood back, who let the women and children go to the boats, that died. There died among us on the shore something of the fierce greed of bitterness, something of the sharp hatred of passion, something of the mad lust of revenge and of knife-edge competition. Though we are not aware of it, perhaps, we are not quite the people that we were before out of the mystery an awful hand was laid upon us all, and what we had thought the colossal power of wealth was in a twinkling shown to be no more than the strength of an infant's little finger, or the twining tendril of a plant.

"Lest we forget; lest we forget!"

WHERE MANHOOD PERISHED NOT

Where cross the lines of forty north
   And fifty-fourteen west
There rolls a wild and greedy sea
   With death upon its crest
No stone or wreath from human hands
   Will ever mark the spot
Where fifteen hundred men went down,
   But Manhood perished not.

Old Ocean takes but little heed
   Of human tears or woe.
No shafts adorn the ocean graves,
   Nor weeping willows grow.
Nor is there need of marble slab
   To keep in mind the spot
Where noble men went down to death,
   But Manhood perished not!

Those men who looked on death and smiled,
   And trod the crumbling deck,
Have saved much more than precious lives

THE MAJESTIC HYMN PLAYED BY THE TITANIC BAND
AS THE VESSEL SANK

AUTUMN 8.7.8.7. D.

Louis von Esch, c. 1810

God of mercy and compassion, Look with pity on my pain;

Hear a mournful, broken spirit Prostrate at Thy feet complain;

Many are my foes and mighty; Strength to conquer I have none

Nothing can uphold my goings But Thy blessed Self alone. AMEN

Saviour, look on Thy beloved,
　Triumph over all my foes;
Turn to heavenly joy my mourning,
　Turn to gladness all my woes;
Live or die, or work or suffer,
　Let my weary soul abide,
In all changes whatsoever,
　Sure and steadfast by Thy side.

When temptations fierce assault me,
　When my enemies I find,
Sin and guilt, and death and Satan,
　All against my soul combined,
Hold me up in mighty waters,
　Keep my eyes on things above—
Rightousness, divine atonement,
　Peace and everlasting love.

WHERE MANHOOD PERISHED NOT.

From out that awful wreck.
Though countless joys and hopes and fears
   Were shattered at a breath,
'Tis something that the name of Man
   Did not go down to death.

'Tis not an easy thing to die,
   E'en in the open air,
Twelve hundred miles from home and friends,
   In a shroud of black despair.
A wreath to crown the brow of man,
   And hide a former blot
Will ever blossom o'er the waves
   Where Manhood perished not.

LOWERING OF THE LIFE-BOATS FROM THE TITANIC

It is easy to understand why the accounts of different eye-witnesses as to what occurred during these tragic moments differ so radically when it is remembered that the Titanic was equal to several city blocks in length, and the boats were leaving from widely separated points. It is not difficult to understand the excitement and panic which reigned, according to some of the survivors, as the life-boats were being filled.

PASSENGERS LEAVING THE TITANIC IN THE LIFE-BOATS

The agony and despair which possessed the occupants of these boats as they were carried away from the doomed giant, leaving husbands and brothers behind, is almost beyond description. It is little wonder that the strain of these moments, with the physical and mental suffering which followed during the early morning hours, left many of the women still hysterical when they reached New York.

CHAPTER VIII

THE CALL FOR HELP HEARD

THE VALUE OF THE WIRELESS—OTHER SHIPS ALTER THEIR COURSE—RESCUERS ON THE WAY.

W E have struck an iceberg. Badly damaged. Rush aid."
Seaward and landward, J. G. Phillips, the Titanic's wireless man, had hurled the appeal for help. By fits and starts—for the wireless was working unevenly and blurringly—Phillips reached out to the world, crying the Titanic's peril. A word or two, scattered phrases, now and then a connected sentence, made up the message that sent a thrill of apprehension for a thousand miles east, west and south of the doomed liner.

The early despatches from St. John's, Cape Race, and Montreal, told graphic tales of the race to reach the Titanic, the wireless appeals for help, the interruption of the calls, then what appeared to be a successful conclusion of the race when the Virginian was reported as having reached the giant liner.

MANY LINES HEAR THE CALL

Other rushing liners besides the Virginian heard the call and became on the instant something more than cargo carriers and passenger greyhounds. The big Baltic, 200 miles to the eastward and westbound, turned again to save life, as she when her sister of the White Star fleet, the Republic, was cut down in a fog in January, 1909. The Titanic's mate, the Olympic, the mightiest of the seagoers save the Titanic herself, turned in her tracks. All along the northern lane the miracle of the wireless worked for the distressed and sinking White Star ship. The Hamburg-American Cincinnati, the Parisian from Glasgow, the North German Lloyd Prinz Friedrich Wilhelm, the Hamburg-American liners Prinz Adelbert and Amerika, all heard the C. Q. D. and the rapid, condensed explanation of what happened.

VIRGINIAN IN DESPERATE HASTE

But the Virginian was nearest, barely 170 miles away, and was the first to know of the Titanic's danger. She went about and headed under forced draught for the spot indicated in one of the last of Phillips' messages—latitude 41.46 N. and longitude 50.14 W. She was a fast ship, the Allan liner, and her wireless told the story of how she stretched through the night to get up to the Titanic in time. There was need for all the power of her engines and all the experience and skill of her captain. The final fluttering Marconigrams that were released from the Titanic made it certain that the great ship with 2340 souls aboard was filling and in desperate peril.

Further out at sea was the Cunarder, Carpathia, which left New York for the Mediterranean on April 13th. Round she went and plunged back westward to take a hand in saving life. And the third steamship within short sailing of the Titanic was the Allan liner Parisian away to the eastward, on her way from Glasgow to Halifax.

While they sped in the night with all the drive that steam could give them, the Titanic's call reached to Cape Race and the startled operator there heard at midnight a message which quickly reached New York:

"Have struck an iceberg. We are badly damaged. Titanic latitude 41.46 N., 50.14 W."

Cape Race threw the appeal broadcast wherever his apparatus could carry.

Then for hours, while the world waited for a crumb of news as to the safety of the great ship's people, not one thing more was known save that she was drifting, broken and helpless and alone in the midst of a waste of ice. And it was not until seventeen hours after the Titanic had sunk that the words came out of the air as to her fate. There was a confusion and tangle of messages—a jumble of rumors. Good tidings were trodden upon by evil. And no man knew clearly what was taking place in that stretch of waters where the giant icebergs were making a mock of all that the world knew best in shipbuilding.

TITANIC SENT OUT NO MORE NEWS

It was at 12.17 A.M., while the Virginian was still plunging eastward, that all communication from the Titanic ceased. The Virginian's operator, with the Virginian's captain at his elbow, fed the air with blue flashes in a desperate effort to know what was happening to the crippled liner, but no message came back. The last word from the Titanic was that she was sinking. then the sparking became fainter. The call was dying to nothing. The Virginian's operator labored over a blur of signals. It was hopeless. So the Allan ship strove on, fearing that the worst had happened.

It was this ominous silence that so alarmed the other vessels hurrying to the Titanic and that caused so much suspense.

CHAPTER IX

IN THE DRIFTING LIFE-BOATS

SORROW AND SUFFERING—THE SURVIVORS SEE THE TITANIC GO
DOWN WITH THEIR LOVED ONES ON BOARD—A NIGHT OF AGONIZ-
ING SUSPENSE—WOMEN HELP TO ROW—HELP ARRIVES—PICKING
UP THE LIFE-BOATS.

SIXTEEN boats were in the procession which entered on the
terrible hours of rowing, drifting and suspense. Women
wept for lost husbands and sons, sailors sobbed for the ship
which had been their pride. Men choked back tears and sought
to comfort the widowed. Perhaps, they said, other boats might
have put off in another direction. They strove, though none too
sure themselves, to convince the women of the certainty that a
rescue ship would appear.

In the distance the Titanic looked an enormous length, her
great bulk outlined in black against the starry sky, every port-
hole and saloon blazing with light. It was impossible to think anything could be wrong with such a leviathan, were it not for that
ominous tilt downwards in the bows, where the water was now
up to the lowest row of port-holes. Presently, about 2 A.M., as
near as can be determined, those in the life-boats observed her
settling very rapidly; with the bows and the bridge completely
under water, and concluded it was now only a question of minutes before she went. So it proved. She slowly tilted straight on

end with the stern vertically upwards, and as she did, the lights in the cabins and saloons, which until then had not flickered for a moment, died out, came on again for a single flash, and finally went altogether. At. the same time the machinery roared down through the vessel with a rattle and a groaning that could be heard for miles, the weirdest sound surely that could be heard in the middle of the ocean, a thousand miles away from land. But this was not yet quite the end.

TITANIC STOOD UPRIGHT

To the amazement of the awed watchers in the life-boats, the doomed vessel remained in that upright position for a time estimated at five minutes; some in the boat say less, but it was certainly some minutes that at least 150 feet of the Titanic towered up above the level of the sea and loomed black against the sky.

SAW LAST OF BIG SHIP

Then with a quiet, slanting dive she disappeared beneath the waters, and the eyes of the helpless spectators had looked for the last time upon the gigantic vessel on which they had set out from Southampton. And there was left to the survivors only the gently heaving sea, the life-boats filled with men and women in every conceivable condition of dress and undress, above the perfect sky of brilliant stars with not a cloud, all tempered with a bitter cold that made each and woman long to be one of the crew who toiled away with the oars and kept themselves warm thereby—a curious, deadening, bitter cold unlike anything they had felt before.

"ONE LONG MOAN"

And then with all these there fell on the ear the most appalling noise that human being has ever listened to—the cries of hundreds of fellow-beings struggling in the icy cold water, crying for help with a cry that could not be answered.

Third Officer Herbert John Pitman, in charge of one of the

boats, described this cry of agony in his testimony before the Senatorial Investigating Committee, under the questioning of Senator Smith:

"I heard no cries of distress until after the ship went down," he said.

"How far away were the cries from your life-boat?"

"Several hundred yards, probably, some of them."

"Describe the screams."

"Don't, sir, please! I'd rather not talk about it."

"I'm sorry to press it, but what was it like? Were the screams spasmodic?"

"It was one long continuous moan."

The witness said the moans and cries continued an hour.

Those in the life-boats longed to return and pick up some of the poor drowning souls, but they feared this would mean swamping the boats and a further loss of life.

Some of the men tried to sing to keep the women from hearing the cries, and rowed hard to get away from the scene of the wreck, but the memory of those sounds will be one of the things the rescued found it difficult to forget.

The waiting sufferers kept a lookout for lights, and several times it was shouted that steamers' lights were seen, but they turned out to be either a light from another boat or a star low down on the horizon. It was hard to keep up hope.

WOMEN TRIED TO COMMIT SUICIDE

"Let me go back—I want to go back to my husband—I'll jump from the boat if you don't," cried an agonized voice in one life-boat.

"You can do no good by going back—other lives will be lost if you try to do it. Try to calm yourself for the sake of the living. It may be that your husband will be picked up somewhere by one of the fishing boats."

The woman who pleaded to go back, according to Mrs. Vera Dick, of Calgary, Canada, later tried to throw herself from the life-boat. Mrs. Dick, describing the scenes in the life-boats, said there were half a dozen women in that one boat who tried to commit suicide when they realized that the Titanic had gone down.

"Even in Canada, where we have such clear nights," said Mrs. Dick, "I have never seen such a clear sky. The stars were very bright and we could see the Titanic plainly, like a great hotel on the water. Floor after floor of the lights went out as we watched. It was horrible, horrible. I can't bear to think about it. From the distance, as we rowed away, we could hear the band playing 'Nearer, My God to Thee.'

"Among the life-boats themselves, however, there were scenes just as terrible, perhaps, but to me nothing could outdo the tragic grandeur with which the Titanic went to its death. To realize it, you would have to see the Titanic as I saw it the day we set sail—with the flags flying and the bands playing. Everybody on board was laughing and talking about the Titanic being the biggest and most luxurious boat on the ocean and being unsink-able. To think of it then and to think of it standing out there in the night, wounded to death and gasping for life, is almost too big for the imagination.

SCANTILY CLAD WOMEN IN LIFE-BOATS

"The women on our boat were in nightgowns and bare feet— some of them—and the wealthiest women mingled with the poorest immigrants. One immigrant woman kept shouting: 'My God, my poor father! He put me in this boat and would not save himself. Oh, why didn't I die, why didn't I die? Why can't I die now?'

"We had to restrain her, else she would have jumped over-board. It was simply awful. Some of the men apparently had said they could row just to get into the boats. We paid no attention to cowardice, however. We were all busy with our own troubles. My heart simply bled for the women who were separated from their husbands.

"The night was frightfully cold, although clear. We had to

huddle together to keep warm. Everybody drank sparingly of the water and ate sparingly of the bread. We did not know when we would be saved. Everybody tried to remain cool, except the poor creatures who could think of nothing but their own great loss. Those with the most brains seemed to control themselves best."

PHILADELPHIA WOMEN WONDERS

How Mrs. George D. Widener, whose husband and son perished after kissing her good-bye and helping her into one of the boats, rowed when exhausted seamen were on the verge of collapse, was told by Emily Geiger, maid of Mrs. Widener, who was saved with her.

The girl said Mrs. Widener bravely toiled throughout the night and consoled other women who had broken down under the strain.

Mrs. William E. Carter and Mrs. John B. Thayer were in the same life-boat and worked heroically to keep it free from the icy menace. Although Mrs. Thayer's husband remained aboard the Titanic and sank with it, and although she had no knowledge of the safety of her son until they met, hours later, aboard the Carpathia, Mrs. Thayer bravely labored at the oars throughout the night.

In telling of her experience Mrs. Carter said:

"When I went over the side with my children and got in the boat there were no seamen in it. Then came a few men, but there were oars with no one to use them. The boat had been filled with passengers, and there was nothing else for me to do but to take an oar.

"We could see now that the time of the ship had come. She was sinking, and we were warned by cries from the men above to pull away from the ship quickly. Mrs. Thayer, wife of the vice-president of the Pennsylvania Railroad, was in my boat, and she, too, took an oar.

"It was cold and we had no time to clothe ourselves with warm overcoats. The rowing warmed me. We started to pull away from the ship. We could see the dim outlines of the decks above, but we could not recognize anybody."

MANY WOMEN ROWING

Mrs. William R. Bucknell's account of the part women played in the rowing is as follows:

"There were thirty-five persons in the boat in which the captain placed me. Three of these were ordinary seamen, supposed to manage the boat, and a steward.

"One of these men seemed to think that we should not start away from the sinking ship until it could be learned whether the other boats would accommodate the rest of the women. He seemed to think that more could be crowded into ours, if necessary.

" 'I would rather go back and go down with the ship than leave under these circumstances,' he cried.

"The captain shouted to him to obey orders and to pull for a little light that could just be discerned miles in the distance. I do not know what this little light was. It may have been a passing fishing vessel, which, of course could not know our predicament. Anyway, we never reached it.

"We rowed all night, I took an oar and sat beside the Countess de Rothes. Her maid had an oar and so did mine. The air was freezing cold and it was not long before the only man that appeared to know anything about rowing commenced to complain that his hands were freezing. A woman back of him handed him a shawl from about her shoulders.

"As we rowed we looked back at the lights of the Titanic. There was not a sound from her, only the lights began to get lower and lower, and finally she sank. Then we heard a muffled explosion and a dull roar caused by the great suction of water.

"There was not a drop of water on our boat. The last minute before our boat was launched Captain Smith threw aboard a bag of bread. I took the precaution of taking a good drink of water before we started, so I suffered no inconvenience from thirst."

Mrs. Lucien Smith, whose young husband perished, was another heroine. It is related by survivors that she took turns at the oars, and then, when the boat was in danger of sinking, stood ready to plug a hole with her finger if the cork stopper became loose.

In another boat Mrs. Cornell and her sister, who had a slight knowledge of rowing, took turns at the oars as did other women.

The boat in which Mrs. J. J. Brown, of Denver, Col., was saved contained only three men in all, and only one rowed. He was a half-frozen seaman who was tumbled into the boat at the last minute. The woman wrapped him in blankets and set him at an oar to start his blood. The second man was too old to be of any use. The third was a coward.

Strange to say, there was room in this boat for ten more people. Ten brave men would have received the warmest welcome of their lives if they had been there. The coward, being a quartermaster and the assigned head of the boat, sat in the stern and steered. He was terrified, and the women had to fight against his pessimism while they tugged at the oars.

The women sat two at each oar. One held the oar in place, the other did the pulling. Mrs. Brown coached them and cheered them on. She told them that the exercise would keep the chill out of their veins, and she spoke hopefully of the likelihood that some vessel would answer the wireless calls. Over the frightful danger of the situation the spirit of this woman soared.

THE PESSIMIST

And the coward sat in his stern seat, terrified, his tongue loosened with fright. He assured them there was no chance in the world. He had had fourteen years' experience, and he knew. First, they would have to row one and a half miles at least to get out of the sphere of the suction, if they did not want to go down. They would be lost, and nobody would ever find them.

"Oh, we shall be picked up sooner or later," said some of the braver ones. No, said the man, there was no bread in the boat, no water; they would starve—all that big boatload wandering the high seas with nothing to eat, perhaps for days.

"Don't," cried Mrs. Brown. "Keep that to yourself, if you feel that way. For the sake of these women and children, be a man. We have a smooth sea and a fighting chance. Be a man."

But the coward only knew that there was no compass and no chart aboard. They sighted what they thought was a fishing smack on the horizon, showing dimly in the early dawn. The man at the rudder steered toward it, and the women bent to their oars again. They covered several miles in this way—but the smack faded into the distance. They could not see it any longer. And the coward said that everything was over.

They rowed back nine weary miles. Then the coward thought they must stop rowing, and lie in the trough of the waves until the Carpathia should appear. The women tried it for a few moments, and felt the cold creeping into their bodies. Though exhausted from the hard physical labor they thought work was better than freezing.

"Row again!" commanded Mrs. Brown.

"No, no, don't," said the coward.

"We shall freeze," cried several of the women together. "We must row. We have rowed all this time. We must keep on or freeze."

When the coward still demurred, they told him plainly and once for all that if he persisted in wanting them to stop rowing, they were going to throw him overboard and be done with him for good. Something about the look in the eye of that Mississippi-bred oarswoman, who seemed such a force among her fellows, told him that he had better capitulate. And he did.

COUNTESS ROTHES AN EXPERT OARSWOMAN

Miss Alice Farnam Leader, a New York physician, escaped from the Titanic on the same boat which carried the Countess Rothes. "The countess is an expert oarswoman," said Doctor Leader, "and thoroughly at home on the water. She practically took command of our boat when it was found that the seaman who had been placed at the oars could not row skillfully. Several of the women took their place with the countess at the oars and rowed in turns, while the weak and unskilled stewards sat quietly in one end of the boat."

MEN COULD NOT ROW

"With nothing on but a nightgown I helped row one of the boats for three hours," said Mrs. Florence Ware, of Bristol, England.

"In our boat there were a lot of women, a steward and a fireman. None of the men knew anything about managing a small boat, so some of the women who were used to boats took charge.

"It was cold and I worked as hard as I could at an oar until we were picked up. There was nothing to eat or drink on our boat."

DEATH ON THE LIFE-BOATS

"The temperature must have been below freezing," testified another survivor, "and neither men nor women in my boat were warmly clothed. Several of them died. The officer in charge of the life-boat decided it was better to bury the bodies. Soon they were weighted so they would sink and were put overboard. We could also see similar burials taking place from other life-boats that were all around us."

GAMBLERS WERE POLITE

In one boat were two card sharps. With the same cleverness that enabled them to win money on board they obtained places in the boats with the women.

In the boat with the gamblers were women in their nightgowns and women in evening dress. None of the boats were properly equipped with food, but all had enough bread and water to keep the rescued from starving until the expected arrival of help.

To the credit of the gamblers who managed to escape, it should be said that they were polite and showed the women every cour-

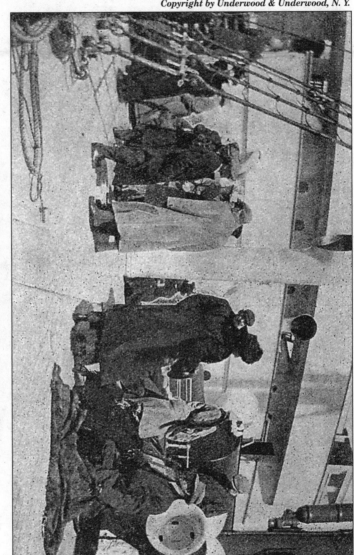
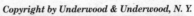

SURVIVORS OF THE GREAT TITANIC MARINE DISASTER

The first authentic photograph, taken by Miss Bernice Palmer, who was on board the Carpathia, showing rescued passengers standing in groups discussing their terrible experiences. The women of the party were supplied with wraps by the women members on board the rescue ship. This picture was taken one hour after the rescued passengers were taken aboard ship.

COLONEL AND MRS. JOHN JACOB ASTOR

Mrs. Astor, neé Miss Madeline Force, was rescued. Colonel Astor who bravely refused to take a place in the life-boats, went down with the Titanic.

tesy. All they wanted was to be sure of getting in a boat. That once accomplished, they reverted to their habitual practice of politeness and suavity. They were even willing to do a little manual labor, refusing to let women do any rowing.

The people on that particular boat were a sad group. Fathers had kissed their daughters good-bye and husbands had parted from their wives. The card sharps, however, philosophized wonderfully about the will of the Almighty and how strange His ways. They said that one must be prepared for anything; that good always came from evil, and that every cloud had a silvery lining.

"Who knows?" said one. "It may be that everybody on board will be saved." Another added: "Our duty is to the living. You women owe it to your relatives and friends not to allow this thing to wreck your reason or undermine your health." And they took pains to see that all the women who were on the life-boat had plenty of covering to keep them from the icy blasts of the night.

HELP IN SIGHT

The survivors were in the life-boats until about 5.30 A.M. About 3 A.M. faint lights appeared in the sky and all rejoiced to see what was supposed to be the coming dawn, but after watching for half an hour and seeing no change in the intensity of the light, the disappointed sufferers realized it was the Northern Lights. Presently low down on the horizon they saw a light which slowly resolved itself into a double light, and they watched eagerly to see if the two lights would separate and so prove to be only two of the boats, or whether these lights would remain together, in which case they should expect them to be the lights of a rescuing steamer.

To the inexpressible joy of all, they moved as one! Immediately the boats were swung around and headed for the lights. Someone shouted: "Now, boys, sing!" and everyone not too weak broke into song with "Row for the shore, boys." Tears came to the eyes of all as they realized that safety was at hand. The song was sung, but it was a very poor imitation of the real thing, for quavering voices make poor songs. A cheer was given next, and that was better—you can keep in tune for a cheer.

THE "LUCKY THIRTEEN"

"Our rescuer showed up rapidly, and as she swung round we saw her cabins all alight, and knew she must be a large steamer. She was now motionless and we had to row to her. Just then day broke, a beautiful quiet dawn with faint pink clouds just above the horizon, and a new moon whose crescent just touched the horizon. 'Turn your money over, boys,' said our cheery steersman, 'that is, if you have any with you,' he added.

"We laughed at him for his superstition at such a time, but he countered very neatly by adding: 'Well, I shall never say again that 13 is an unlucky number; boat 13 has been the best friend we ever had.' Certainly the 13 superstition is killed forever in the minds of those who escaped from the Titanic in boat 13.

"As we neared the Carpathia we saw in the dawning light what we thought was a full-rigged schooner standing up near her, and presently behind her another, all sails set, and we said: 'They are fisher boats from the Newfoundland bank and have seen the steamer lying to and are standing by to help.' But in another five minutes the light shone pink on them and we saw they were icebergs towering many feet in the air, huge, glistening masses, deadly white, still, and peaked in a way that had easily suggested a schooner. We glanced round the horizon and there were others wherever the eye could reach. The steamer we had to reach was surrounded by them and we had to make a detour to reach her, for between her and us lay another huge berg."

A WONDERFUL DAWN

Speaking of the moment when the Carpathia was sighted, Mrs. J. J. Brown, who had cowed the driveling quartermaster, said:

"Then, knowing that we were safe at last, I looked about me. The most wonderful dawn I have ever seen came upon us. I have just returned from Egypt. I have been all over the world, but I have never seen anything like this. First the gray and then the flood of light. Then the sun came up in a ball of red fire. For the first time we saw where we were. Near us was open water, but on every side was ice. Ice ten feet high was everywhere, and to the right and left and back and front were icebergs. Some of them were mountain high. This sea of ice was forty miles wide, they told me. We did not wait for the Carpathia to come to us, we rowed to it. We were lifted up in a sort of nice little sling that was lowered to us. After that it was all over. The passengers of the Carpathia were so afraid that we would not have room enough that they gave us practically the whole ship to ourselves."

It had been learned that some of the passengers, in fact all of the women passengers of the Titanic who were rescued, refer to "Lady Margaret," as they called Mrs. Brown, as the strength of them all.

TRANSFERRING THE RESCUED

Officers of the Carpathia report that when they reached the scene of the Titanic's wreck there were fifty bodies or more floating in the sea. Only one mishap attended the transfer of the rescued from the life-boats. One large collapsible life-boat, in which thirteen persons were seated, turned turtle just as they were about to save it, and all in it were lost.

THE DOG HERO

Not the least among the heroes of the Titanic disaster was Rigel, a big black Newfoundland dog, belonging to the first officer, who went down with the ship. But for Rigel the fourth boat picked up might have been run down by the Carpathia. For three hours he swam in the icy water where the Titanic went down, evidently looking for his master, and was instrumental in guiding the boatload of survivors to the gangway of the Carpathia.

Jonas Briggs, a seaman aboard the Carpathia, now has Rigel and told the story of the dog's heroism. The Carpathia was moving slowly about, looking for boats, rafts or anything which might be afloat. Exhausted with their efforts, weak from lack of food and exposure to the cutting wind, and terror-stricken, the men and women in the fourth boat had drifted under the Carpathia's starboard bow. They were dangerously close to the steamship, but too weak to shout a warning loud enough to reach the bridge.

The boat might not have been seen were it not for the sharp barking of Rigel, who was swimming ahead of the craft and valiantly announcing his position. The barks attracted the attention of Captain Rostron, and he went to the starboard end of the bridge to see where they came from and saw the boat. He immediately ordered the engines stopped, and the boat came alongside the starboard gangway.

Care was taken to get Rigel aboard, but he appeared little affected by his long trip through the ice-cold water. He stood by the rail and barked until Captain Rostron called Briggs and had him take the dog below.

A THRILLING ACCOUNT OF RESCUE

Mr. Wallace Bradford, of San Francisco, a passenger aboard the Carpathia, gave the following thrilling account of the rescue of the Titanic's passengers.

"Since half-past four this morning I have experienced one of those never-to-be-forgotten circumstances that weighs heavy on my soul and which shows most awfully what poor things we mortals are. Long before this reaches you the news will be flashed that the Titanic has gone down and that our steamer, the Carpathia, caught the wireless message when seventy-five miles away, and so far we have picked up twenty boats estimated to contain about 750 people.

"None of us can tell just how many, as they have been bustled to various staterooms and to the dining saloons to be warmed up. I was awakened by unusual noises and imagined that I smelled smoke. I jumped up and looked out of my port-hole, and saw a huge iceberg looming up like a rock off shore. It was not white, and I was positive that it was a rock, and the thought flashed through my mind, how in the world can we be near a rock when we are four days out from New York in a southerly direction and in mid-ocean.

"When I got out on deck the first man I encountered told me that the Titanic had gone down and we were rescuing the passengers. The first two boats from the doomed vessel were in sight making toward us, Neither of them was crowded. This was accounted for later by the fact that it was impossible to get many to leave the steamer, as they would not believe that she was going down. It was a glorious, clear morning and a quiet sea. Off to the starboard was a white area of ice plain, from whose even surface rose mammoth forts, castles and pyramids of solid ice almost as real as though they had been placed there by the hand of man.

"Our steamer was hove to about two and a half miles from the edge of this huge iceberg. The Titanic struck about 11.20 P.M. and did not go down until two o'clock. Many of the passengers were in evening dress when they came aboard our ship, and most of these were in a most bedraggled condition. Near me as I write is a girl about eighteen years old in a fancy dress costume of bright colors, while in another seat near by is a woman in a white dress trimmed with lace and covered with jaunty blue flowers.

"As the boats came alongside after the first two all of them contained a very large proportion of women. In fact, one of the boats had women at the oars, one in particular containing, as near as I could estimate, about forty-five women and only about six men. In this boat two women were handling one of the oars. All of the engineers went down with the steamer. Four bodies have been brought aboard. One is that of a fireman, who is said to have been shot by one of the officers because he refused to obey orders. Soon after I got on deck I could, with the aid of my glasses, count seven boats headed our way, and they continued to come up to half past eight o'clock. Some were in sight for a long time and

moved very slowly, showing plainly that the oars were being handled by amateurs or by women.

"No baggage of any kind was brought by the survivors. In
fact, the only piece of baggage that reached the Carpathia from
the Titanic is a small closed trunk about twenty-four inches
square, evidently the property of an Irish female immigrant.
While some seemed fully dressed, many of the men having their
overcoats and the women sealskin and other coats, others came
just as they had jumped from their berths, clothed in their paja-
mas and bath robes."

THE SORROW OF THE LIVING

Of the survivors in general it may be said that they escaped
death and they gained life. Life is probably sweet to them as it
is to everyone, but what physical and mental torture has been
the price of life to those who were brought back to land on the
Carpathia—the hours in life-boats, amid the crashing of ice, the
days of anguish that have succeeded, the horrors of body and
mind still experienced and never to be entirely absent until death
affords them its relief.

The thought of the nation to-day is for the living. They need
our sympathy, our consolation more than do the dead, and, perhaps, in the majority of the cases they need our protecting care
as well.

CHAPTER X

ON BOARD THE CARPATHIA

AID FOR THE SUFFERING AND HYSTERICAL—BURYING THE
DEAD—VOTE OF THANKS TO CAPTAIN ROSTRON OF THE CARPA-
THIA—IDENTIFYING THOSE SAVED—COMMUNICATING WITH
LAND—THE PASSAGE TO NEW YORK.

IF THE scenes in the life-boats were tear-bringing, hardly
less so was the arrival of the boats at the Carpathia with
their bands of terror-stricken, grief-ridden survivors, many
of them too exhausted to know that safety was at hand. Watchers
on the Carpathia were moved to tears.

"The first life-boat reached the Carpathia about half-past five
o'clock in the morning," recorded one of the passengers on the
Carpathia. "And the last of the sixteen boats was unloaded before
nine o'clock. Some of the life-boats were only half filled, the first
one having but two men and eleven women, when it had accommodations for at least forty. There were few men in the boats.
The women were the gamest lot I have ever seen. Some of the
men and women were in evening clothes, and others among those
saved had nothing on but night clothes and raincoats."

After the Carpathia had made certain that there were no more
passengers of the Titanic to be picked up, she threaded her way
out of the ice fields for fifty miles. It was dangerous work, but it
was managed without trouble.

AID FOR THE SUFFERING AND HYSTERICAL

The shrieks and cries of the women and men picked up in life-boats by the Carpathia were horrible. The women were clothed only in night robes and wrappers. The men were in their night garments. One was lifted on board entirely nude. All the passengers who could bear nourishment were take into the dining rooms and cabins by Captain Rostron and given food and stimulants. Passengers of the Carpathia gave up their berths and staterooms to the survivors.

As soon as they were landed on the Carpathia many of the women became hysterical, but on the whole they behaved splendidly. Men and women appeared to be stunned all day Monday, the full force of the disaster not reaching them until Tuesday night. After being wrapped up in blankets and filled with brandy and hot coffee, the first thoughts were of their husbands and those at home. Most of them imagined that their husbands had been picked up by other vessels, and they began flooding the wireless rooms with messages. It was almost certain that those who were not on board the Carpathia had gone down to death.

One of the most seriously injured was a woman who had lost both her children. Her limbs had been severely torn, but she was very patient.

WOMEN SEEKING NEWS

In the first cabin library women of wealth and refinement mingled their grief and asked eagerly for news of the possible arrival of a belated boat, or a message from other steamers telling of the safety of their husbands. Mrs. Henry B. Harris, wife of a New York theatrical manager, checked her tears long enough to beg that some message of hope be sent to her father-in-law. Mrs. G. Thorne, Miss Marie Young, Mrs. Emil Taussig and her daughter, Ruth, Mrs. Martin Rothschild, Mrs. William Augustus Spencer, Mrs. J. Stewart White and Mrs. Walter M. Clark were a few of those who lay back, exhausted, on the leather cushions and told in shuddering sentences of their experiences.

Mrs. John Jacob Astor and the Countess of Rothes had been taken to staterooms soon after their arrival on shipboard.

Before noon, at the captain's request, the first cabin passengers of the Titanic gathered in the saloon and the passengers of other classes in corresponding places on the rescue ship. Then the collecting of names was begun by the purser and the stewards. A second table was served in both cabins for the new guests, and the Carpathia's second cabin, being better filled than its first, the second class arrivals had be to sent to the steerage.

TEARS THEIR ONLY RELIEF

Mrs. Jacques Futrelle, wife of the novelist, herself a writer of note, sat dry eyed in the saloon, telling her friends that she had given up hope for her husband. She joined with the rest in inquiries as to the chances of rescue by another ship, and no one told her what soon came to be the fixed opinion of the men— that all those saved were on the Carpathia.

"I feel better," Mrs. Futrelle said hours afterward, "for I can cry now."

Among the men conversation centered on the accident and the responsibility for it. Many expressed the belief that the Titanic, in common with other vessels had had warning of the ice packs, but that in the effort to establish a record on the maiden run sufficient heed had not been paid to the warnings.

"God knows I'm not proud to be here," said a rich New York man. "I got on a boat when they were about to lower it and when, from delays below, there was no woman to take the vacant place. I don't think any man who was saved is deserving of censure, but I realize that, in contrast with those who went down, we may be viewed unfavorably." He showed a picture of his baby boy as he spoke.

PITIFUL SCENES OF GRIEF

As the day passed the fore part of the ship assumed some degree of order and comfort, but the crowded second cabin and rear decks gave forth the incessant sound of lamentation. A bride of two months sat on the floor and moaned her widowhood. An Italian mother shrieked the name of her lost son.

A girl of seven wept over the loss of her Teddy bear and two dolls while her mother, with streaming eyes, dared not tell the child that her father was lost too, and that the money for which their home in England had been sold had gone down with him. Other children clung to the necks of the fathers who, because carrying them, had been permitted to take the boats.

In the hospital and the public rooms lay, in blankets, several others who had been benumbed by the water. Mrs. Rosa Abbott, who was in the water for hours, was restored during the day. K. Whiteman, the Titanic's barber, who declared he was blown off the ship by the second of the two explosions after the crash, was treated for bruises. A passenger, who was thoroughly dunked before being picked up, caused much amusement on this ship, soon after the doctors were through with him, by demanding a bath.

SURVIVORS AND THE DESTITUTE

Storekeeper Prentice, the last man off the Titanic to reach this ship, was also soon over the effects of his long swim in the icy waters into which he leaped from the poop deck.

The physicians of the Carpathia were praised, as was Chief Steward Hughes, for work done in making the arrivals comfortable and averting serious illness.

Monday night on the Carpathia was one of rest. The wailing and sobbing of the day were hushed as widows and orphans slept. Tuesday, save for the crowded condition of the ship, matters took somewhat their normal appearance.

The second cabin dining room had been turned into a hospital to care for the injured, and the first, second and third class dining rooms were used for sleeping rooms at night for women, while the smoking rooms were set aside for men. All available space was used, some sleeping in chairs and some on the floor, while a few found rest in the bathrooms.

Every cabin had been filled, and women and children were sleeping on the floors in the dining saloon, library and smoking rooms. The passengers of the Carpathia had divided their clothes with the shipwrecked ones until they had at least kept warm. It is true that many women had to appear on deck in kimonos and some in underclothes with a coat thrown over them, but their lives had been spared and they had not thought of dress. Some children in the second cabin were entirely without clothes, but the women had joined together, and with needles and thread they could pick up from passenger to passenger, had made warm clothes out of the blankets belonging to the Carpathia.

WOMEN BEFRIENDED ONE ANOTHER

The women aboard the Carpathia did what they could by word and act to relieve the sufferings of the rescued. Most of the survivors were in great need of clothing, and this the women of the Carpathia supplied to them as long as their surplus stock held out.

J. A. Shuttleworth, of Louisville, Ky., befriended Mrs. Lucien Smith, whose husband went down with the Titanic; Mrs. Smith was formerly Miss Eloise Hughes, daughter of Representative and Mrs. James A. Hughes, of Huntington, W. Va., and was on her wedding trip. Mr. Shuttleworth asked her if there wasn't something he could do for her. She said that all the money she had was lost on the Titanic, so Mr. Shuttleworth gave her $50.

DEATHS ON THE CARPATHIA

Two of the rescued from the Titanic died from shock and expo-

sure before they reached the Carpathia, and another died a few
minutes after being taken on board. The dead were W. H. Hoyte,
first cabin; Abraham Hormer, third class, and S. C. Sirbert, steward, and they were buried at sea the morning of April 15th, latitude 41.14 north, longitude 51.24 west. P. Lyon, able seaman,
died and was buried at sea the following morning.

An assistant steward lost his mind upon seeing one of the
Titanic's rescued firemen expire after being lifted to the deck of
the Carpathia.

An Episcopal bishop and a Catholic priest from Montreal read
services of their respective churches over the dead.

The bodies were sewed up in sacks, heavily weighted at the
feet, and taken to an opening in the side of the ship on the lower
deck not far above the water line. A long plank tilted at one end
served as the incline down which the weighted sacks slid into
the sea.

"After we got the Titanic's passengers on board our ship,"
said one of the Carpathia's officers, "it was a question as to
where we should take them. Some said the Olympic would
come out and meet us and take them on to New York, but others
said they would die if they had to be lowered again into small
boats to be taken up by another, so we finally turned toward
New York, delaying the Carpathia's passengers eight days in
reaching Gibralter."

SURVIVORS WATCH NEW BOATS

There were several children on board, who had lost their parents—one baby of eleven months with a nurse who, coming on
board the Carpathia with the first boat, watched with eager-
ness and sorrow for each incoming boat but, to no avail. The
parents had gone down.

There was a woman in the second cabin who lost seven
children out of ten, and there were many other losses quite as
horrible.

DIAGRAM OF THE TITANIC'S ARRANGEMENT AND EQUIPMENT

The Titanic was far and away the largest and finest vessel ever built, excepting only her sister-ship, the Olympic. Her dimensions were: Length, 882 ½ feet; Beam, 92 feet; Depth (from keel to tops of funnels), 175 feet; Tonnage, 45,000. Her huge hull, divided into thirty watertight compartments, contained nine steel decks, and provided accommodation for 2,500 passengers, besides a crew of 890.

UPPER DECK OF THE TITANIC, LOOKING FORWARD

MR. ISMAY "PITIABLE SIGHT"

Among the rescued ones who came on board the Carpathia was the president of the White Star Line.

"Mr. Ismay reached the Carpathia in about the tenth life-boat," said an officer. "I didn't know who he was, but afterward heard the others of the crew discussing his desire to get something to eat the minute he put his foot on the deck. The steward who waited on him, McGuire, from London, says Mr. Ismay came dashing into the dining room, and throwing himself in a chair, said: "Hurry, for God's sake, and get me something to eat; I'm starved. I don't care what it costs or what it is, bring it to me."

"McGuire brought Mr. Ismay a load of stuff and when he had finished it, he handed McGuire a two dollar bill. 'Your money is no good on this ship,' McGuire told him. 'Take it,' insisted Mr. Ismay, shoving the bill in McGuire's hand. 'I am well able to afford it. I will see to it that the boys of the Carpathia are well rewarded for this night's work.' This promise started McGuire making inquiries as to the identity of the man he had waited on. Then we learned that he was Mr. Ismay. I did not see Mr. Ismay after the first few hours. He must have kept to his cabin."

A passenger on the Carpathia said there was no wonder that none of the wireless telegrams addressed to Mr. Ismay were answered until the one that he sent yesterday afternoon to his line, the White Star.

"Mr. Ismay was beside himself," said this woman passenger, "and on most of the voyage after we had picked him up he was being quieted with opiates on orders of the ship's doctor."

FIVE DOGS AND ONE PIG SAVED

"Five women saved their pet dogs, carrying them in their arms. Another woman saved a little pig, which she said was her mascot. Though her husband is an Englishman and she lives in England she is an American and was on her way to visit her folks here. How she cared for the pig aboard ship I do not know, but she carried it up the side of the ship in a big bag. I did not mind the dogs so much, but it seemed to me to be too much when a pig was saved and human beings went to death.

"It was not until noon on Monday that we cleared the last of the ice, and Monday night a dense fog came up and continued until the following morning, then a strong wind, a heavy sea, a thunderstorm and a dense fog Tuesday night caused some uneasiness among the more unnerved, the fog continuing all of Tuesday.

"A number of whales were sighted as the Carpathia was clearing the last of the ice, one large one being close by, and all were spouting like geysers.

VOTE OF THANKS TO CARPATHIA

"On Tuesday afternoon a meeting of the uninjured survivors was called in the main saloon for the purpose of devising means of assisting the more unfortunate, many of whom had lost relatives and all their personal belongings, and thanking Divine Providence for their deliverance. The meeting was called to order and Mr. Samuel Goldenberg was elected chairman. Resolutions were then passed thanking the officers, surgeons, passengers and crew of the Carpathia for their splendid services in aiding the rescued and like resolutions for the admirable work done by the officers, surgeons and crew of the Titanic.

"A committee was then appointed to raise funds on board the Carpathia to relieve the immediate wants of the destitute and assist them in reaching their destinations and also to present a loving cup to the officers of the Carpathia and also a loving cup to the surviving officers of the Titanic.

"Mr. T. G. Frauenthal, of New York was made chairman of the Committee on Subscriptions.

"A committee, consisting of Mrs. J. J. Brown, Mrs. William Bucknell and Mrs. George Stone, was appointed to look after the destitute. There was a subscription taken up and up to Wednesday the amount contributed totaled $15,000.

"The work of the crew on board the Carpathia in rescuing was most noble and remarkable, and these four days that the ship has been overcrowded with its 710 extra passengers could not have been better handled. The stewards have worked with undying strength—although one was overcome with so much work and died and was put to his grave at sea.

"I have never seen or felt the benefits of such royal treatment. I have heard the captain criticised because he did not answer telegrams, but all that I can say is that he showed us every possible courtesy, and if we had been on our own boats, having paid our fares there, we could not have had better food or better accommodations.

"Men who had paid for the best staterooms on the Carpathia left their rooms so that we might have them. They fixed up beds in the smoking rooms, and mattresses everywhere. All the women who were rescued were given the best staterooms, which were surrendered by the regular passengers. None of the regular passengers grumbled because their trip to Europe was interrupted, nor did they complain that they were put to the inconvenience of receiving hundreds of strangers.

"The women on board the Carpathia were particularly kind. It shows that for every cruelty of nature there is a kindness, for every misfortune there is some goodness. The men and women took up collections on board for the rescued steerage passengers. Mrs. Astor, I believe, contributed $2000, her check being cashed by the Carpathia. Altogether something like $15,000 was collected and all the women were provided with sufficient money to reach their destination after they were landed in New York."

Under any other circumstances the suffering would have been intolerable. But the Good Samaritans on the Carpathia gave many women heart's-ease.

The spectacle on board the Carpathia on the return trip to New York at times was heartrending, while at other times those on board were quite cheerful.

CHAPTER XI

PREPARATIONS ON LAND TO RECEIVE THE SUFFERERS

POLICE ARRANGEMENTS—DONATIONS OF MONEY AND SUPPLIES—
HOSPITALS AND AMBULANCES MADE READY—PRIVATE HOUSES
THROWN OPEN—WAITING FOR THE CARPATHIA TO ARRIVE—THE
SHIP SIGHTED!

NEW YORK CITY, touched to the heart by the great ocean calamity and desiring to do what it could to lighten the woes and relieve the sufferings of the piti- ful little band of men and women rescued from the Titanic, opened both its heart and its purse.

The most careful and systematic plans were made for the reception and transfer to homes, hotels or institutions of the Titanic's survivors. Mayor Gaynor, with Police Commissioner Waldo, arranged to go down the bay on the police boat Patrol, to come up with the Carpathia and take charge of the police arrangements at the pier.

In anticipation of the enormous number that would, for a variety of reasons, creditable or otherwise, surge about the Cunard pier at the coming of the Carpathia, Mayor Gaynor and the police commissioner had seen to it that the streets should be rigidly sentineled by continuous lines of policemen. Under Inspector George McClusky, the man of most experience, perhaps, in handling large crowds, there were 200 men, including twelve mounted men and a number in citizens' clothes. For two blocks to the north, south and east of the docks lines were established through which none save those bearing passes from the Government and the Cunard Line could penetrate.

With all arrangements made that experience or information could suggest, the authorities settled down to await the docking of the Carpathia. No word had come to either the White Star Line or the Cunard Line, they said, that any of the Titanic's people had died on that ship or that bodies had been recovered from the sea, but in the afternoon Mayor Gaynor sent word to the Board of Coroners that it might be well for some of that body to meet the incoming ship. Coroners Feinberg and Holtzhauser with Coroner's Physician Weston arranged to go down the bay on the Patrol, while Coroner Hellenstein waited at the pier. An undertaker was notified to be ready if needed. Fortunately there was no such need.

EVERY POSSIBLE MEASURE THOUGHT OF

Every possible measure of relief for the survivors that could be thought of by officials of the city, of the Federal Government, by the heads of hospitals and the Red Cross and relief societies was arranged for. The Municipal Lodging House, which has accommodations for 700 persons, agreed to throw open its doors and furnish lodging and food to any of the survivors as long as they should need it. Commissioner of Charities Drummond did not know, of course, just how great the call would be for the services of his department. He went to the Cunard pier to direct his part of the work in person. Meanwhile he had twenty ambulances ready for instant movement on the city's pier at the foot of East Twenty-sixth Street. They were ready to take patients to the reception hospital connected with Bellevue or the Metropolitan Hospital on Blackwell's Island. Ambulances from the Kings County Hospital in Brooklyn were also there to do their share. All the other hospitals in the city stood ready to take the Titanic's people and those that had ambulances promised to send them. The Charities ferryboat, Thomas S. Brennan, equipped as a hospital craft, lay off the department pier with nurses and physicians ready to be called to the Cunard pier on the other side of the city. St. Vincent's Hospital had 120 beds ready, New York Hospital twelve, Bellevue and the reception hospital 120 and Flower Hospital twelve.

The House of Shelter maintained by the Hebrew Sheltering and Immigrant Aid Society announced that it was able to care for at least fifty persons as long as might be necessary. The German Society of New York, the Irish Immigrant Society, the Italian Society, the Swedish Immigrant Society and the Young Men's Christian Association were among the organizations that also offered to see that no needy survivor would go without shelter.

Mrs. W. A. Bastede, whose husband was a member of the staff of St. Luke's Hospital, offered to the White Star Line the use of the newly opened ward at St. Luke's, which could accommodate from thirty to sixty persons. She said the hospital would send four ambulances with nurses and doctors and that she had collected clothing enough for fifty persons. The line accepted her offer and said that the hospital would be kept informed as to what was needed.

A trustee of Bellevue also called at the White Star offices to offer ambulances. He said that five or six, with two or three doctors and nurses on each, would be sent to the pier if required.

Many other hospitals as well as individuals called at the mayor's office, expressing willingness to take in anybody that should be sent to them A woman living in Fiftieth Street just off Fifth Avenue wished to put her home at the disposal of the survivors. D. H. Knott, of 102 Waverley Place, told the mayor that he could take care of 100 and give them both food and lodging at the Arlington, Holly and Earl Hotels. Commissioner Drummond visited the City Hall and arranged with the mayor the plans for the relief to be extended directly by the city. Mr. Drummond said that omnibuses would be provided to transfer passengers from the ship to the Municipal Lodging House.

MRS. VANDERBILT'S EFFORTS

Mrs. W. K. Vanderbilt, Jr., spent the day telephoning to her friends, asking them to let their automobiles be used to meet the Carpathia and take away those who needed surgical care. It was announced that as a result of Mrs. Vanderbilt's efforts 100 limousine automobiles and all the Fifth Avenue and Riverside Drive automobile buses would be at the Cunard pier.

Immigration Commissioner Williams said that he would be at the pier when the Carpathia came in. There was to be no inspection of immigrants at Ellis Island. Instead, the commissioner sent seven or eight inspectors to the pier to do their work there and he asked them to do it with the greatest possible speed and the least possible bother to the shipwrecked aliens. The immigrants who had no friends to meet them were to be provided for until their cases could be disposed of. Mr. Williams thought that some of them who had lost everything might have to be sent back to their homes. Those who were to be admitted to the United States were to be cared for by the Women's Relief Committee.

RED CROSS RELIEF

Robert W. de Forest, chairman of the Red Cross Relief Committee of the Charity Organization Society, after conferring with Mayor Gaynor, said that in addition to an arrangement that all funds received by the mayor should be paid to Jacob H. Schiff, the New York treasurer of the American Red Cross, the committee had decided that it could turn over all the immediate relief work to the Women's Relief Committee.

The Red Cross Committee announced that careful plans had been made to provide for every possible emergency.

The emergency committee received a telegram that Ernest P. Bicknell, director of the American Red Cross, was coming from Washington. The Red Cross Emergency Relief Committee was to have several representatives at the pier to look out for the passengers on the Carpathia. Mr. Persons and Dr. Devine were to be there and it was planned to have others.

The Salvation Army offered, through the mayor's office, accommodation for thirty single men at the Industrial Home, 533 West Forty-eighth Street, and for twenty others at its hotel, 18 Chatham Square. The army's training school at 124 West Fourteenth Street was ready to take twenty or thirty survivors. R. H. Farley, head of the White Star Line's third class department, said that the line would give all the steerage passengers railroad tickets to their destination.

Mayor Gaynor estimated that more than 5000 persons could be accommodated in quarters offered through his orders. Most of these offers of course would have to be rejected. The mayor also said that Colonel Conley of the Sixty-ninth Regiment offered to turn out his regiment to police the pier, but it was thought that such service would be unnecessary.

CROWDS AT THE DOCKS

Long before dark on Thursday night a few people passed the police lines and with a yellow card were allowed to go on the dock; but reports had been published that the Carpathia would not be in till midnight, and by 8 o'clock there were not more than two hundred people on the pier. In the next hour the crowd with passes trebled in number. By 9 o'clock the pier held half as many as it could comfortably contain. The early crowd did not contain many women relatives of the survivors. Few nervous people could be seen, but here and there was a woman, usually supported by two male escorts, weeping softly to herself.

On the whole it was a frantic, grief-crazed crowd. Laborers rubbed shoulders with millionaires.

The relatives of the rich had taxicabs waiting outside the docks. The relatives of the poor went there on foot in the rain, ready to take their loved ones.

A special train was awaiting Mrs. Charles M. Hays, widow of the president of the Grand Trunk Railroad. A private car also awaited Mrs. George D. Widener.

EARLY ARRIVALS AT PIER

Among the first to arrive at the pier was a committee from the Stock Exchange, headed by R. H. Thomas, and composed of Charles Knoblauch, B. M. W. Baruch, Charles Holzderber and J. Carlisle. Mr. Thomas carried a long black box which contained $5000 in small bills, which was to be handed out to the needy steerage survivors of the Titanic as they disembarked.

With the early arrivals at the pier were the relatives of Frederick White, who was not reported among the survivors, though Mrs. White was; Harry Mock, who came to look for a brother and sister; and Vincent Astor, who arrived in a limousine with William A. Dobbyn, Colonel Astor's secretary, and two doctors. The limousine was kept waiting outside to take Mrs. Astor to the Astor home on Fifth Avenue.

EIGHT LIMOUSINE CARS

The Waldorf-Astoria had sent over eight limousine cars to convey to the hotel these survivors:

Mrs. Mark Fortune and three daughters, Mrs. Lucien P. Smith, Mrs. J. Stewart White, Mrs. Thornton Davidson, Mrs. George C. Douglass, Mrs. George D. Widener and maid, Mrs. George Wick, Miss Bonnell, Miss E. Ryerson, Mrs. Susan P. Ryerson, Mrs. Arthur Ryerson, Miss Mary Wick, the Misses Howell, Mrs. John P. Snyder and Mr. and Mrs. D. E. Bishop.

THIRTY-FIVE AMBULANCES AT THE PIER

At one time there were thirty-five ambulances drawn up outside the Cunard pier. Every hospital in Manhattan, Brooklyn and the Bronx was represented. Several of the ambulances came from as far north as the Lebanon Hospital, in the Bronx, and the Brooklyn Hospital, in Brooklyn.

Accompanying them were seventy interns and surgeons from the staffs of the hospitals, and more than 125 male and female nurses.

St. Vincent's sent the greatest number of ambulances, at one time, eight of them from this hospital being in line at the pier.

Miss Eva Booth, direct head of the Salvation Army, was at the pier, accompanied by Miss Elizabeth Nye and a corps of her officers, ready to aid as much as possible. The Sheltering Society and various other similar organizations also were represented, all ready to take care of those who needed them.

An officer of the Sixty-ninth Regiment, N. G. N. Y., offered the White Star Line officials, the use of the regiment's armory for any of the survivors.

Mrs. Thomas Hughes, Mrs. August Belmont and Mgrs. Lavelle and McMahon, of St. Patrick's Cathedral, together with a score of black-robed Sisters of Charity, representing the Association of Catholic Churches, were on the pier long before the Carpathia was made fast, and worked industriously in aiding the injured and ill.

The Rev. Dr. William Carter, pastor of the Madison Avenue Reformed Church, was one of those at the pier with a private ambulance awaiting Miss Sylvia Caldwell, one of the survivors, who is known in church circles as a mission worker in foreign fields.

FREE RAILROAD TRANSPORTATION

The Pennsylvania Railroad sent representatives to the pier, who said that the railroad had a special train of nine cars in which it would carry free any passenger who wanted to go immediately to Philadelphia or points west. The Pennsylvania also had eight taxicabs at the pier for conveyance of the rescued to the Pennsylvania Station, in Thirty-third Street.

Among those who later arrived at the pier before the Carpathia docked were P. A. B. Widener, of Philadelphia, two women relatives of J. B. Thayer, William Harris, Jr., the theatrical man, who was accompanied by Dr. Dinkelspiel, and Henry Arthur Jones, the playwright.

RELATIVES OF SAVED AND LOST

Commander Booth, of the Salvation Army, was there especially to meet Mrs. Elizabeth Nye and Mrs. Rogers Abbott, both Titanic survivors. Mrs. Abbott's two sons were supposed to be among the lost. Miss Booth had received a cablegram from London saying that other Salvation Army people were on the Titanic. She was eager to get news of them.

Also on the pier was Major Blanton, U. S. A., stationed at Washington, who was waiting for tidings of Major Butt, supposedly at the instance of President Taft.

Senator William A. Clark and Mrs. Clark were also in the company. Dr. John R. MacKenty was waiting for Mr. and Mrs. Henry S. Harper. Ferdinand W. Roebling and Carl G. Roebling, cousins of Washington A. Roebling, Jr., whose name is among the list of dead, went to the pier to see what they could learn of his fate.

J. P. Morgan, Jr., arrived at the pier about half an hour before the Carpathia docked. He said he had many friends on the Titanic and was eagerly awaiting news of all of them.

Fire Commissioner Johnson was there with John Peel, of Atlanta, Ga., a brother of Mrs. Jacques Futrelle. Mrs. Futrelle has a son twelve years old in Atlanta, and a daughter Virginia, who has been in school in the North and is at present with friends in this city, ignorant of her father's death.

A MAN IN HYSTERICS

There was one man in that sad waiting company who startled those near him about 9 o'clock by dancing across the pier and back. He seemed to be laughing, but when he was stopped it was found that he was sobbing. He said that he had a relative on the Titanic and had lost control of his nerves.

H. H. Brunt, of Chicago, was at the gangplank waiting for A.

Saalfeld, head of the wholesale drug firm of Sparks, White & Co., of London, who was coming to this country on the Titanic on a business trip and whose life was saved.

WAITING FOR CARPATHIA

During the afternoon and evening tugboats, motor boats and even sailing craft, had been waiting off the Ambrose Light for the appearance of the Carpathia.

Some of the waiting craft contained friends and anxious relatives of the survivors and those reported as missing.

The sea was rough and choppy, and a strong east wind was blowing. There was a light fog, so that it was possible to see at a distance of only a few hundred yards. This lifted later in the evening.

First to discover the incoming liner with her pitiful cargo was one of the tugboats. From out of the mist there loomed far out at sea the incoming steamer.

RESCUE BOAT SIGHTED

"Liner ahead!" cried the lookout on the tug to the captain.

"She must be the Carpathia," said the captain, and then he turned the nose of his boat toward the spot on the horizon.

Then the huge black hull and one smokestack could be distinguished.

"It's the Carpathia," said the captain. "I can tell her by the stack."

The announcement sent a thrill through those who heard it. Here, at the gate of New York, was a ship whose record for bravery and heroic work would be a familiar name in history.

MRS. LUCIEN P. SMITH

Formerly Miss Eloise Hughes, daughter of Representative and Mrs. James A. Hughes, of West Virginia. Mrs. Smith and her husband went to a watery grave. Mr. and Mrs. Smith were married only a few months earlier.

MAJOR ARCHIBALD BUTT

Military Aide to President Taft. Of Major Butt, who was one of the victims of the Titanic, one of the survivors said: "Major Butt was the real leader in all of that rescue work.

CHAPTER XII

THE TRAGIC HOME-COMING

THE CARPATHIA REACHES NEW YORK—AN INTENSE AND DRAMATIC MOMENT—HYSTERICAL REUNIONS AND CRUSHING DISAPPOINTMENTS AT THE DOCK—CARING FOR THE SUFFERERS—FINAL REALIZATION THAT ALL HOPE FOR OTHERS IS FUTILE—LIST OF SURVIVORS—ROLL OF THE DEAD.

IT was a solemn moment when the Carpathia heaved in sight. There she rested on the water, a blur of black-huge, mysterious, awe-inspiring—and yet withal a thing to send thrills of pity and then of admiration through the beholder.

It was a few minutes after seven o'clock when she arrived at the entrance to Ambrose Channel. She was coming fast steaming at better than fifteen knots an hour, and she was sighted long before she was expected. Except for the usual side and mast-head lights she was almost dark, only the upper cabins showing a glimmer here and there.

Then began a period of waiting, the suspense of which proved almost too much for the hundreds gathered there to greet friends and relatives or to learn with certainty at last that those for whom they watched would never come ashore.

There was almost complete silence on the pier. Doctors and nurses, members of the Women's Relief Committee, city and government officials, as well as officials of the line, moved nervously about.

Seated where they had been assigned beneath the big customs letters corresponding to the initials of the names of the survivors they came to meet, sat the mass of 2000 on the pier.

Women wept, but they wept quietly, not hysterically, and the sound of the sobs made many times less noise than the hum and bustle which is usual on the pier among those awaiting an incoming liner.

Slowly and majestically the ship slid through the water, still bearing the details of that secret of what happened and who perished when the Titanic met her fate.

Convoying the Carpathia was a fleet of tugs bearing men and women anxious to learn the latest news. The Cunarder had been as silent for days as though it, too, were a ship of the dead. A list of survivors had been given out from its wireless station and that was all. Even the approximate time of its arrival had been kept a secret.

NEARING PORT

There was no response to the hail from one tug, and as others closed in, the steamship quickened her speed a little and left them behind as she swung up the channel.

There was an exploding of flashlights from some of the tugs, answered seemingly by sharp stabs of lightning in the northwest that served to accentuate the silence and absence of light aboard the rescue ship. Five or six persons, apparently members of the crew or the ship's officers, were seen along the rail; but otherwise the boat appeared to be deserted.

Off quarantine the Carpathia slowed down and, hailing the immigration inspection boat, asked if the health officer wished to board. She was told that he did, and came to a stop while Dr. O'Connell and two assistants climbed on board. Again the newspaper men asked for some word of the catastrophe to the Titanic, but there was no answer, and the Carpathia continued toward her pier.

As she passed the revenue cutter Mohawk and the derelict destroyer Seneca anchored off Tompkinsville the wireless on the Government vessels was seen to flash, but there was no answering spark from the Carpathia. Entering the North River she laid her course close to the New Jersey side in order to have room to swing into her pier.

By this time the rails were lined with men and women. They were very silent. There were a few requests for news from those on board and a few answers to questions shouted from the tugs.

The liner began to slacken her speed, and the tugboat soon was alongside. Up above the inky blackness of the hull figures could be made out, leaning over the port railing, as though peering eagerly at the little craft which was bearing down on the Carpathia.

Some of them, perhaps, had passed through that inferno of the deep sea which sprang up to destroy the mightiest steamship afloat.

"Carpathia, ahoy!" was shouted through a megaphone.

There was an interval of a few seconds, and then, "Aye, aye," came the reply.

"Is there any assistance that can be rendered?" was the next question.

"Thank you, no," was the answer in a tone that carried emotion with it. Meantime the tugboat was getting nearer and nearer to the Carpathia, and soon the faces of those leaning over the railing could be distinguished.

TALK WITH SURVIVORS

More faces appeared, and still more.

A woman who called to a man on the tugboat was asked, "Are you one the Titanic survivors?"

"Yes," said the voice, hesitatingly.

"Do you need help?"

"No," after a pause.

"If there is anything you want done it will be attended to."

"Thank you. I have been informed that my relatives will meet me at the pier."

"Is it true that some of the life-boats sank with the Titanic?"

"Yes. There was some trouble in manning them. They were not far enough away from her."

All of this questioning and receiving replies was carried on with the greatest difficulty. The pounding of the liner's engines, the washing of the sea, the tugboat's engines, made it hard to understand the woman's replies.

ALL CARED FOR ON BOARD

"Were the women properly cared for after the crash?" she was asked.

"Oh, yes," came the shrill reply. "The men were brave—very brave." Here her voice broke and she turned and left the railing, to reappear a few moments later and cry:

"Please report me as saved."

"What name?" was asked. She shouted a name that could not be understood, and, apparently believing that it had been, turned away again and disappeared.

"Nearly all of us are very ill," cried another woman. Here several other tugboats appeared, and those standing at the railing were besieged with questions.

"Did the crash come without warning?" a voice on one of the smaller boats megaphoned.

"Yes," a woman answered. "Most of us had retired. We saved a few of our belongings."

"How long did it take the boat to sink?" asked the voice.

TITANIC CREW HEROES

"Not long," came the reply. "The crew and the men were very brave. Oh, it is dreadful—dreadful to think of!"

"Is Mr. John Jacob Astor on board?"

"No."

"Did he remain on the Titanic after the collision?"

"I do not know."

Questions of this kind were showered at the few survivors who stood at the railing, but they seemed too confused to answer them intelligibly, and after replying evasively to some they would disappear.

RUSHES ON TO DOCK

"Are you going to anchor for the night?" Captain Rostron was asked by megaphone as his boat approached Ambrose Light. It was then raining heavily.

"No," came the reply. "I am going into port. There are sick people on board."

"We tried to learn when she would dock," said Dr. Walter Kennedy, head of the big ambulance corps on the mist-shrouded pier, "and we were told it would not be before mid-night and that most probably it would not be before dawn to-morrow. The childish deception that has been practiced for days by the people who are responsible for the Titanic has been carried up to the very moment of the landing of the survivors."

She proceeded past the Cunard pier, where 2000 persons were waiting her, and steamed to a spot opposite the White Star piers at Twenty-first Street.

The ports in the big inclosed pier of the Cunard Line were opened, and through them the waiting hundreds, almost frantic with anxiety over what the Carpathia might reveal, watched her as with nerve-destroying leisure she swung about in the river, dropping over the life-boats of the Titanic that they might be taken to the piers of the White Star Line.

THE TITANIC LIFE-BOATS

It was dark in the river, but the lowering away of the life-boats could be seen from the Carpathia's pier, and a deep sigh arose from the multitude there as they caught this first glance of anything associated with the Titanic.

Then the Carpathia started for her own pier. As she approached it the ports on the north side of pier 54 were closed that the Carpathia might land there, but through the two left open to accommodate the forward and after gangplanks of the big liner the watchers could see her looming larger and larger in the darkness till finally she was directly alongside the pier.

As the boats were towed away the picture taking and shouting of questions began again. John Badenoch, a buyer for Macy & Co., called down to a representative of the firm that neither Mr. nor Mrs. Isidor Straus were among the rescued on board the Carpathia. An officer of the Carpathia called down that 710 of the Titanic's passengers were on board, but refused to reply to other questions.

The heavy hawsers were made fast without the customary shouting of ship's officers and pier hands. From the crowd on the pier came a long, shuddering murmur. In it were blended sighs and hundreds of whispers. The burden of it all was: "Here they come."

ANXIOUS MEN AND WOMEN

About each gangplank a portable fence had been put in place, marking off some fifty feet of the pier, within which stood one hundred or more customs officials. Next to the fence, crowded close against it, were anxious men and women, their gaze strained for a glance of the first from the ship, their mouths opened to draw their breaths in spasmodic, quivering gasps, their very bodies shaking with suppressed excitement, excitement which only the suspense itself was keeping in subjection.

These were the husbands and wives, children, parents, sweethearts and friends of those who had sailed upon the Titanic on its maiden voyage.

They pressed to the head of the pier, marking the boats of the wrecked ship as they dangled at the side of the Carpathia and were revealed in the sudden flashes of the photographers upon the tugs. They spoke in whispers, each group intent upon its own sad business. Newspaper writers, with pier passes showing in their hat bands, were everywhere.

A sailor hurried outside the fence and disappeared, apparently on a mission for his company. There was a deep-drawn sigh as he walked away, shaking his head toward those who peered eagerly at him. Then came a man and woman of the Carpathia's own passengers, as their orderly dress showed them to be.

Again a sigh like a sob swept over the crowd, and again they turned back to the canopied gangplank.

THE FIRST SURVIVORS

Several minutes passed and then out of the first cabin gangway, tunneled by a somber awning, streamed the first survivors. A young woman, hatless, her light brown hair disordered and the leaden weight of crushing sorrow heavy upon eyes and sensitive mouth, was in the van. She stopped, perplexed, almost ready to drop with terror and exhaustion, and was caught by a customs official.

"A survivor?" he questioned rapidly, and a nod of the head answering him, he demanded:

"Your name."

The answer given, he started to lead her toward that section of the pier where her friends would be waiting.

When she stepped from the gangplank there was quiet on the pier. The answers of the woman could almost be heard by those fifty feet away, but as she staggered, rather than walked, toward the waiting throng outside the fence, a low wailing sound arose from the crowd.

"Dorothy, Dorothy!" cried a man from the number. He broke through the double line of customs inspectors as though it was composed of wooden toys and caught the woman to his breast. She opened her lips inarticulately, weakly raised her arms and would have pitched forward upon her face had she not been supported. Her fair head fell weakly to one side as the man picked her up in his arms, and, with tears streaming down his face, stalked down the long avenue of the pier and down the long stairway to a waiting taxicab.

The wailing of the crowd—its cadences, wild and weird—grew steadily louder and louder till they culminated in a mighty shriek, which swept the whole big pier as though at the direction of some master hand.

RUMORS AFLOAT

The arrival of the Carpathia was the signal for the most sensational rumors to circulate through the crowd on the pier.

First, Mrs. John Jacob Astor was reported to have died at 8.06 o'clock, when the Carpathia was on her way up the harbor.

Captain Smith and the first engineer were reported to have shot themselves when they found that the Titanic was doomed to sink. Afterward it was learned that Captain Smith and the engineer went down with their ship in perfect courage and coolness.

Major Archibald Butt, President Taft's military aide, was said to have entered into an agreement with George D. Widener, Colonel John Jacob Astor and Isidor Straus to kill them first and then shoot himself before the boat sank. It was said that this agreement had been carried out. Later it was shown that, like many other men on the ship, they had gone down without the exhibition of a sign of fear.

MRS. CORNELL SAFE

Magistrate Cornell's wife and her two sisters were among the first to leave the ship. They were met at the first cabin pier entrance by Magistrate Cornell and a party of friends. None of the three women had hats. One of those who met them was Magistrate Cornell's son. One of Mrs. Cornell's sisters was overheard to remark that "it would be a dreadful thing when the ship began really to unload."

The three women appeared to be in a very nervous state. Their hair was more or less dishevelled. They were apparently fully dressed save for their hats. Clothing had been supplied them in their need and everything had been done to make them comfortable. One of the party said that the collision occurred at 9.45.

Following closely the Cornell party was H. J. Allison, of Montreal, who came to meet his family. One of the party, who was weeping bitterly as he left the pier, explained that the only one of the family that was rescued was the young brother.

MRS. ASTOR APPEARED

In a few minutes young Mrs. Astor with her maid appeared. She came down the gangplank unassisted. She was wearing a white sweater. Vincent Astor and William Dobbyn, Colonel Astor's secretary, greeted her and hurried her to a waiting limousine which contained clothing and other necessaries of which it was thought she might be in need. The young woman was white-faced and silent. Nobody cared to intrude upon her thoughts. Her stepson said little to her. He did not feel like questioning her at such a time, he said.

LAST SEEN OF COLONEL ASTOR

Walter M. Clark, a nephew of the senator, said that he had seen Colonel Astor put his wife in a boat, after assuring her that he would soon follow her in another. Mr. Clark and others said that Colonel and Mrs. Astor were in their suite when the crash came, and that they appeared quietly on deck a few minutes afterward.

Here and there among the passengers of the Carpathia and from the survivors of the Titanic the story was gleaned of the rescue. Nothing in life will ever approach the joy felt by the hundreds who were waiting in little boats on the spot where the Titanic foundered when the lights of the Carpathia were first distinguished. That was at 4 o'clock on Monday morning.

DR. FRAUENTHAL WELCOMED

Efforts were made to learn from Dr. Henry Frauenthal something about the details of how he was rescued. Just then, or as he was leaving the pier, beaming with evident delight, he was surrounded by a big crowd of his friends.

"There's Harry! There he is!" they yelled and made a rush for him.

All the doctor's face that wasn't covered with red beard was aglow with smiles as his friends hugged him and slapped him on the back. They rushed him off bodily through the crowd and he too was whirled home.

A SAD STORY

How others followed—how heartrending stories of partings and of thrilling rescues were poured out in an amazing stream— this has all been told over and over again in the news that for days amazed, saddened and angered the entire world. It is the story of a disaster that nations, it is hoped, will make impossible in the years to come.

In the stream of survivors were a peer of the realm, Sir Cosmo Duff Gordon, and his secretary, side by side with plain Jack Jones, of Birmingham, able seaman, millionaires and paupers, women with bags of jewels and others with nightgowns their only property.

MORE THAN SEVENTY WINDOWS

More than seventy widows were in the weeping company. The only large family that was saved in its entirety was that of the Carters, of Philadelphia. Contrasting with this remarkable salvage of wealthy Pennsylvanians was the sleeping eleven-months-old baby of the Allisons, whose father, mother and sister went down to death after it and its nurse had been placed in a life-boat.

Millionaire and pauper, titled grandee and weeping immigrant, Ismay, the head of the White Star Company, and Jack

Jones from the stoke hole were surrounded instantly. Some would gladly have escaped observation. Every man among the survivors acted as though it were first necessary to explain how he came to be in a life-boat. Some of the stories smacked of Munchausen. Others were as plain and unvarnished as a pike staff. Those that were most sincere and trustworthy had to be fairly pulled from those who gave their sad testimony.

Far into the night the recitals were made. They were told in the rooms of hotels, in the wards of hospitals and upon trains that sped toward saddened homes. It was a symposium of horror and heroism, the like of which has not been known in the civilized world since man established his dominion over the sea.

STEERAGE PASSENGERS

The two hundred and more steerage passengers did not leave the ship until 11 o'clock. They were in a sad condition. The women were without wraps and the few men there were wore very little clothing. A poor Syrian woman who said she was Mrs. Habush, bound for Youngstown, Ohio, carried in her arms a six-year-old baby girl. This woman had lost her husband and three brothers. "I lost four of my men folks," she cried.

TWO LITTLE BOYS

Among the survivors who elicited a large measure of sympathy were two little French boys who were dropped, almost naked, from the deck of the sinking Titanic into a life-boat. From what place in France did they come and to what place in the New World were they bound? There was not one iota of information to be had as to the identity of the waifs of the deep, the orphans of the Titanic.

The two baby boys, two and four years old, respectively, were in charge of Miss Margaret Hays, who is a fluent speaker of French, and she had tried vainly to get from the lisping lips of the two little ones some information that would lead to the finding of their relatives.

Miss Hays, also a survivor of the Titanic, took charge of the almost naked waifs on the Carpathia. She became warmly attached to the two boys, who unconcernedly played about, not understanding the great tragedy that had come into their lives.

The two little curly-heads did not understand it all. Had not their pretty nineteen-year-old foster mother provided them with pretty suits and little white shoes and playthings a-plenty? Then, too, Miss Hays had a Pom dog that she brought with her from Paris and which she carried in her arms when she left the Titanic and held to her bosom through the long night in the life-boat, and to which the children became warmly attached. All three became aliens on an alien shore.

Miss Hays, unable to learn the names of the little fellows, had dubbed the older Louis and the younger "Lump." "Lump" was all that his name implies, for he weighed almost as much as his brother. They were dark-eyed and brown curly-haired children, who knew how to smile as only French children can.

On the fateful night of the Titanic disaster and just as the last boats were pulling away with their human freight, a man rushed to the rail holding the babes under his arms. He cried to the passengers in one of the boats and held the children aloft. Three or four sailors and passengers held up their arms. The father dropped the older boy. He was safely caught. Then he dropped the little fellow and saw him folded in the arms of a sailor. Then the boat pulled away.

The last seen of the father, whose last living act was to save his babes, he was waving his hand in a final parting. Then the Titanic plunged to the ocean's bed.

BABY TRAVERS

Still more pitiable in one way was the lot of the baby survivor, eleven-months-old Travers Allison, the only member of a family of four to survive the wreck. His father, H. J. Allison, and mother and Lorraine, a child of three, were victims of the catastrophe. Baby Travers, in the excitement following the crash, was separ-

WHITE STAR STEAMER TITANIC GYMNASIUM

CAPTAIN A. H. ROSTRON

Commander of the Carpathia, which rescued the survivors of the Titanic from the life-boats in the open sea and brought them to New York. After the Senatorial Investigating Committee had examined Captain Rostron, at which time this specially posed photograph was taken, Senator William Alden Smith, chairman of the committee, said of Captain Rostron: "His conduct of the rescue shows that he is not only an efficient seaman, but one of nature's noblemen."

ated from the rest of the family just before the Titanic went down. With the party were two nurses and a maid.

Major Arthur Peuchen, of Montreal, one of the survivors, standing near the little fellow, who, swathed in blankets, lay blinking at his nurse, described the death of Mrs. Allison. She had gone to the deck without her husband, and, frantically seeking him, was directed by an officer to the other side of the ship.

She failed to find Mr. Allison and was quickly hustled into one of the collapsible life-boats, and when last seen by Major Peuchen she was toppling out of the half-swamped boat. J. W. Allison, a cousin of H. J. Allison, was at the pier to care for Baby Travers and his nurse. They were taken to the Manhattan Hotel.

Describing the details of the perishing of the Allison family, the rescued nurse said they were all in bed when the Titanic hit the berg.

"We did not get up immediately," said she, "for we had not thought of danger. Later we were told to get up, and I hurriedly dressed the baby. We hastened up on deck, and confusion was all about. With other women and children we clambered to the life-boats, just as a matter of precaution, believing that there was no immediate danger. In about an hour there was an explosion and the ship appeared to fall apart. We were in the life-boat about six hours before we were picked up."

THE RYERSON FAMILY

Probably few deaths have caused more tears than Arthur Ryerson's, in view of the sad circumstances which called him home from a lengthy tour in Europe. Mr. Ryerson's eldest son, Arthur Larned Ryerson, a Yale student, was killed in an automobile accident Easter Monday, 1912.

A cablegram announcing the death plunged the Ryerson family into mourning and they boarded the first steamship for this country. It happened to be the Titanic, and the death note came near being the cause of the blotting out of the entire family.

The children who accompanied them were Miss Susan P. Ryerson, Miss Emily B. Ryerson and John Ryerson. The latter was 12 years old.

They did not know their son intended to spend the Easter holidays at their home at Haverford, Pa. until they were informed of his death. John Lewis Hoffman, also of Haverford and a student of Yale, was killed with young Ryerson.

The two were hurrying to Philadelphia to escort a fellow student to his train. In turning out of the road to pass a cart the motor car crashed into a pole in front of the entrance to the estate of Mrs. B. Frank Clyde. The college men were picked up unconscious and died in the Bryn Mawr Hospital.

G. Heide Norris of Philadelphia, who went to New York to meet the surviving members of the Ryerson family, told of a happy incident at the last moment as the Carpathia swung close to the pier. There had been no positive information that young "Jack" Ryerson was among those saved—indeed, it was feared that he had gone down with the Titanic, like his father, Arthur Ryerson.

Mr. Norris spoke of the feeling of relief that came over him as, watching from the pier, he saw "Jack" Ryerson come from a cabin and stand at the railing. The name of the boy was missing from some of the lists and for two days it was reported that he had perished.

CAPTAIN ROSTRON'S REPORT

Less than 24 hours after the Cunard Line steamship Carpathia came in as a rescue ship with survivors of the Titanic disaster, she sailed again for the Mediterranean cruise which she originally started upon the previous week. Just before the liner sailed, H. S. Bride, the second Marconi wireless operator of the Titanic, who had both of his legs crushed on a life-boat, was carried off on the shoulders of the ship's officers to St. Vincent's Hospital.

Captain A. H. Rostron, of the Carpathia, addressed an official report, giving his account of the Carpathia's rescue work, to the general manager of the Cunard Line, Liverpool. The report read: "I beg to report that at 12.35 A.M. Monday 18th inst. I was informed of urgent message from Titanic with her position. I immediately ordered ship turned around and put her in course for that position, we being then 58 miles S. 52—E. 'T' from her; had heads of all departments called and issued what I considered the necessary orders, to be in preparation for any emergency.

"At 2.40 A.M. saw flare half a point on port bow. Taking this for granted to be ship, shortly after we sighted our first iceberg. I had previously had lookouts doubled, knowing that Titanic had struck ice, and so took every care and precaution. We soon found ourselves in a field of bergs, and had to alter course several times to clear bergs; weather fine, and clear, light air on sea, beautifully clear night, though dark.

"We stopped at 4 A. M., thus doing distance in three hours and a half, picking up the first boat at 4.10 A.M.; boat in charge of officer, and he reported that Titanic had foundered. At 8.30 A.M. last boat picked up. All survivors aboard and all boats accounted for, viz., fifteen life-boats, one boat abandoned, two Berthon boats alongside (saw one floating upwards among wreckage), and according to second officer (senior officer saved) one Berthon boat had not been launched, it having got jammed, making sixteen life-boats and four Berthon boats accounted for. By the time we had cleared first boat it was breaking day, and I could see all within area of four miles. We also saw that we were surrounded by icebergs, large and small, huge field of drift ice with large and small bergs in it, the ice field trending from N. W. round W. and S. to S. E., as far as we could see either way.

"At 8 A.M. the Leyland S. S. California came up. I gave him the principal news and asked him to search and I would proceed to New York; at 8.50 proceeded full speed while researching over vicinity of disaster, and while we were getting people aboard I gave orders to get spare hands along and swing in all our boats, disconnect the fall and hoist up as many Titanic boats as possible in our davits; also get some on forecastle heads by derricks. We got thirteen lifeboats, six on forward deck and seven in davits. After getting all survivors aboard and while searching I got a clergyman to offer a short prayer of thankfulness for those saved, and also a short burial service for their loss, in saloon.

"Before deciding definitely where to make for, I conferred with Mr. Ismay, and as he told me to do what I thought best, I informed him, I considered New York best. I knew we should require clean blankets, provisions and clean linen, even if we went to the Azores, as most of the passengers saved were women and children, and they hysterical, not knowing what medical attention they might require. I thought it best to go to New York. I also thought it would be better for Mr. Ismay to go to New York or England as soon as possible, and knowing I should be out of wireless communication very soon if I proceeded to Azores, it left Halifax, Boston and New York, so I chose the latter.

"Again, the passengers were all hysterical about ice, and I pointed out to Mr. Ismay the possibilities of seeing ice if I went to Halifax. Then I knew it would be best to keep in touch with land stations as best I could. We have experienced great difficulty in transmitting news, also names of survivors. Our wireless is very poor, and again we have had so many interruptions from other ships and also messages from shore (principally press, which we ignored). I gave instructions to send first all official messages, then names of passengers, then survivors' private messages. We had haze early Tuesday morning for several hours; again more or less all Wednesday from 5.30 A.M. to 5 A.M.; strong south-southwesterly winds and clear weather Thursday, with moderate rough sea.

"I am pleased to say that all survivors have been very plucky. The majority of women, first, second and third class, lost their husbands, and, considering all, have been wonderfully well. Tuesday our doctor reported all survivors physically well. Our first class passengers have behaved splendidly, given up their cabins voluntarily and supplied the ladies with clothes, etc. We all turned out of our cabins and gave them to survivors-saloon, smoking room, library, etc., also being used for sleeping accommodation. Our crew, also turned out to let the crew of the Titanic take their quarters. I am pleased to state that owing to preparations made for the comfort of survivors, none were the worse for exposure, etc. I beg to specially mention how willing and cheerful the whole of the ship's company behaved, receiving the highest praise from everybody. And I can assure you I am very proud to have such a company under my command.

— "A. H. Rostron."

The following list of the survivors and dead contains the latest revisions and corrections of the White Star Line officials, and was furnished by them exclusively for this book.

LIST OF SURVIVORS
FIRST CABIN

Anderson, Harry.
Antoinette, Miss.
Appieranelt, Miss.
Appleton, Mrs. E. D.
Abbott, Mrs. Rose.
Allison, Master, and nurse.
Andrews, Miss Cornelia I.
Allen, Miss. E. W.
Astor, Mrs. John Jacob, and maid.
Aubeart, Mme. N., and maid.

Barratt, Karl B.
Besette, Miss.
Barkworth, A.H.
Bucknell, Mrs. W.
Bowerman, Miss E.
Brown, Mrs. J. J.
Burns, Miss C. M.
Bishop, Mr. and Mrs. D. H.
Blank, H.

Bessina, Miss A.
Baxter, Mrs. James.
Brayton, George.
Bonnell, Miss Lily.
Brown, Mrs. J. M.
Bowen, Miss G. C.
Beckwith, Mr. and Mrs. R. L.
Bisley, Mr. and Mrs.
Bonnell, Miss C.

Cassebeer, Mrs. H. A.
Cardeza, Mrs. J. W.
Candell, Mrs. Churchill.
Case, Howard B.
Camarion, Kenard.
Casseboro, Miss D. D.
Clark, Mrs. W. M.
Chibinace, Mrs. B. C.
Charlton, W. M.
Crosby, Mrs. E. G.

LIST OF SURVIVORS—FIRST CABIN (Continued)

Carter, Miss Lucille.
Calderhead, E. P.
Chandanson, Miss Victorine.
Cavendish, Mrs. Turrell, and
    maid.
Chafee, Mrs. H. I.
Cardeza, Mr. Thomas.
Cummings, Mrs. J.
Chevre, Paul.
Cherry, Miss Gladys.
Chambers, Mr. and Mrs. N. C.
Carter, Mr. and Mrs. W. E.
Carter, Master William.
Compton, Mrs. A. T.
Compton, Miss S. R.
Crosby, Mrs. E. G.
Crosby, Miss Harriet.
Cornell, Mrs. R. C.
Chibnall, Mrs. E.

Douglas, Mrs. Fred.
De Villiers, Mme.
Daniel, Miss Sarah.
Daniel, Robert W.
Davidson, Mr. and Mrs.
    Thornton, and family.
Douglas, Mrs. Walter, and maid.
Dodge, Miss Sarah.
Dodge, Mrs. Washington, and
    son.
Dick, Mr. and Mrs. A. A.
Daniell, H. Haren.
Drachensted, A.
Daly, Peter D.

Endres, Miss Caroline.
Ellis, Miss.
Earnshaw, Mrs. Boulton.
Eustis, Miss E.

Emmock, Philip E.
Flagenheim, Mrs. Antoinette.
Franicatelli, Miss.
Flynn, J. I.
Fortune, Miss Alice.
Fortune, Miss Ethel.
Fortune, Mrs. Mark.
Fortune, Miss Mabel.
Frauenthal, Dr. and Mrs. H. W.
Frauenthal, Mr. and Mrs. T. G.
Frolicher, Miss Margaret.
Frolicher, Max and Mrs.
Frolicher, Miss N.
Futrelle, Mrs. Jacques.

Gracie, Colonel Archibald.
Graham, Mr. and Mrs. William.
Graham, Miss M.
Gordon, Sir Cosmo Duff.
Gordon, Lady.
Gibson, Miss Dorothy.
Goldenberg, Mr. and Mrs.
    Samuel.
Goldenberg, Miss Ella.
Greenfield, Mrs. L. P.
Greenfield, G. B.
Greenfield, William.
Gibson, Mrs. Leonard.
Googht, James.

Haven, Mr. Henry B.
Harris, Mrs. H. B.
Holverson, Mrs. Alex.
Hogeboom, Mrs. J. C.
Hawksford, W. J.
Harper, Henry, and man servant.
Harper, Mrs. H. S.
Hold, Miss J. A.
Hope, Nina.

LIST OF SURVIVORS — FIRST CABIN (Continued)

Hoyt, Mr. and Mrs. Fred.
Horner, Henry R.
Harder, Mr. and Mrs. George.
Hays, Mrs. Charles M., and daughter.
Hippach, Miss Jean.
Hippach, Mrs. Ida S.

Ismay, J. Bruce.

Jenasco, Mrs. J.

Kimball, Mr. and Mrs. Ed. N.
Kennyman, F.A.
Kenchen, Miss Emile.

Longley, Miss G. F.
Leader, Mrs. A. F.
Leahy, Miss Nora.
Lavory, Miss Bertha.
Lines, Mrs. Ernest.
Lines, Miss Mary.
Lindstrom, Mrs. Singird.
Lesneur, Gustave, Jr.

Madill, Miss Georgette A.
Mahan, Mrs.
Melicard, Mme.
Menderson, Miss Letta.
Maimy, Miss Roberta.
Marvin, Mrs. D. W.
Marechell, Pierre.
Maroney, Mrs. R.
Meyer, Mrs. E. I.
Mock, Mr. P. E.
Middle, Mme. M. Olive.
Minahan, Miss Daisy.
Minahan, Mrs. W. E.
McGough, James.

Newell, Miss Alice.
Newell, Miss Madeline.
Newell, Washington.
Newson, Miss Helen.

O'Connell, Miss R.
Ostby, E. C.
Ostby, Miss Helen.
Omund, Fieunam.

Panhart, Miss Ninette.
Pears, Mrs. E.
Pomroy, Miss Ellen.
Potter, Mrs. Thomas, Jr.
Peuchen, Major Arthur.
Peercault, Miss A.

Ryerson, John.
Renago, Mrs. Mamam.
Ranelt, Miss Appie.
Rothschild, Mrs. Lord Martin.
Rosenbaum, Miss Edith.
Rheims, Mr. and Mrs. George.
Rosible, Miss H.
Rothes, Countess.
Robert, Mrs. Edna.
Rolmane, C.
Ryerson, Miss Susan P.
Ryerson, Miss Emily.
Ryerson, Mrs. Arthur, and maid.

Stone, Mrs. George M.
Skeller, Mrs. William.
Segesser, Miss Emma.
Seward, Fred. K.
Shutter, Miss.
Sloper, William T.
Swift, Mrs. F. Joel.
Schabert, Mrs. Paul.
Sheddel, Robert Douglass.

LIST OF SURVIVORS—FIRST CABIN (Continued)

Snyder, Mr. and Mrs. John.
Serepeca, Miss Augusta.
Silverthorn, R. Spencer.
Saalfeld, Adolf.
Stahelin, Max.
Simoinus, Alfonsius.
Smith, Mrs. Lucien P.
Stephenson, Mrs. Walter.
Solomon, Abraham.
Silvey, Mrs. William B.
Stenmel, Mr. and Mrs. Heleery.
Spencer, Mrs. W. A., and maid.
Slayter, Miss Hilda.
Spedden, Mr. and Mrs. F. O.,
  and child.
Steffanson, H. B.
Straus, Mrs., maid of.
Schabert, Mrs. Emma.
Slinter, Mrs. E.
Simmons, A.

Taylor, Miss.
Tucker, Mrs., and maid.
Thayer, Mrs. J. B.
Thayer, J. B., Jr.

Taussig, Miss Ruth.
Taussig, Mrs. E.
Thor, Miss Ella.
Thorne, Mrs. G.
Taylor, Mr. and Mrs. E. Z.
Trout, Miss Jessie.
Tucker, Gilbert.

Woolner, Hugh.
Ward, Miss Anna.
Williams, Richard M., Jr.
Warren, Mrs. F.
Wilson, Miss Helen A.
Williard, Miss C.
Wick, Miss Mary.
Wick, Geo.
Widener, valet of.
Widener, Mrs. George D., and
  maid.
White, Mrs. J. Stuart.

Young, Miss Marie

LIST OF SURVIVORS—SECOND CABIN

Abesson, Mrs. Hanna.
Abbot, Mrs. R.
Argenia, Mrs., and two
  children.
Angel, F.
Angle, William.

Baumthorpe, Mrs. L.
Balls, Mrs. Ada E.
Buss, Miss Kate.

Becker, Mrs. A. O., and three
  children.
Beane, Edward.
Beane, Mrs. Ethel.
Bryhl, Miss D.
Beesley, Mr. L.
Brown, Mr. T. W. S.
Brown, Miss E.
Brown, Mrs.
Benthan, Lillian W.

LIST OF SURVIVORS—SECOND CABIN (Continued)

Bystron, Karolina.
Bright, Dagmar.
Bright, Daisy.

Clarke, Mrs. Ada.
Cameron, Miss C.
Caldwell, Albert F.
Caldwell, Mrs. Sylvan.
Caldwell, Alden, infant.
Cristy, Mr. and Mrs.
Collyer, Mrs. Charlotte.
Collyer, Miss Marjorie.
Christy, Mrs. Alice.
Collet, Stuart.
Christa, Miss Ducia.
Charles, William.
Croft, Millie Mall.

Doling, Mrs. Elsie.
Drew, Mrs. Lulu.
Davis, Mrs. Agnes.
Davis, Miss Mary.
Davis, John M.
Duvan, Florentine.
Duvan, Miss A.
Davidson, Miss Mary.
Doling, Miss Ada.
Driscoll, Mrs. B.
Deystrom, Caroline.

Emcarmacion, Mrs. Rinaldo.

Faunthorpe, Mrs. Lizzie.
Formerly, Miss Ellen.

Garside, Ethel.
Gerrecai, Mrs. Marcy.
Genovese, Angere.

Hart, Mrs. Esther.
Hart, Eva.
Harris, George.
Hewlette, Mrs. Mary.
Hebber, Miss S.
Hoffman, Lola.
Hoffman, Louis.
Harper, Nina.
Hold, Stephen.
Hold, Mrs. Anna.
Hosono, Masubumi.
Hocking, Mr. and Mrs. George.
Hocking, Miss Nellie.
Herman, Mrs. Jane, 2
   daughters.
Healy, Nora.
Hanson, Jennie.
Hamatainen, W.
Hamatainen, Anna.
Harnlin, Anna, and child.

Ilett, Bertha.

Jackson, Mrs. Amy.
Juliet, Luwche.
Jerwan, Mary.
Juhon, Podro.
Jacobson, Mrs.

Keane, Miss Nora H.
Kelly, Mrs. F.
Kantar, Mrs. S.

Leitch, Jessie.
Laroche, Mrs. and Miss
   Simmone.
Laroche, Miss Louise.
Lehman, Bertha.
Launch, Mrs. Alex.

LIST OF SURVIVORS—SECOND CABIN (Continued)

Laniore, Amelia.
Lystrom, Mrs. C.

Mellinger, Elizabeth.
Mellinger, child.
Marshall, Mrs. Kate.
Mallett, A.
Mallett, Mrs. and child.
Mange, Paula.
Mare, Mrs. Florence.
Mellor, W. J.
McDearmont, Miss Lela.
McGowan, Anna.

Nye, Elizabeth.
Nasser, Mrs. Delia.
Nussa, Mrs. A.

Oxenham, Percy J.

Phillips, Alice.
Pallas, Emilio.
Padro, Julian.
Prinsky, Rosa.
Portaluppi, Emilio.
Parsh, Mrs. L.
Plett, B.

Quick, Mrs. Jane.
Quick, Mrs. Vera W.
Quick, Miss Phyllis.

Reinardo, Miss E.
Risdale, Lucy.

Renouf, Mrs. Lily.
Rugg, Miss Emily.
Richards, M.
Rogers, Miss Selina.
Richards, Mrs. Emilia, two
    boys, and Mr. Richards, Jr.

Simpson, Miss.
Sinock, Miss Maude.
Sinkkonnen, Anna.
Smith, Miss Marion.
Silven, Lylle.

Trant, Mrs. J.
Toomey, Miss E.
Troutt, Miss E.
Troutt, Miss Cecilia.

Ware, Miss H.
Watter, Miss N.
Wilhelm, Chas.
Wat, Mrs. A., and two children.
Williams, Richard M., Jr.
Weisz, Mathilde.
Webber, Miss Susie.
Wright, Miss Marion.
Watt, Miss Bessie.
Watt, Miss Bertha.
West, Mrs. E. A.
West, Miss Constance.
West, Miss Barbara.
Wells, Addie.
Wells, Master.
Wells, Miss.

A list of surviving third cabin passengers and crew is omitted owing to the impossibility of obtaining the correct names of many.

ROLL OF THE DEAD

First Cabin

Allison, H. J.
Allison, Mrs., and maid.
Allison, Miss.
Andrews, Thomas.
Artagaveytia, Mr. Ramon.
Astor, Col. J. J., and servant.
Anderson, Walker.

Beattie, T.
Brandeis, E.
Bucknell, Mrs. William, maid of.
Baumann, J.
Baxter, Mr. and Mrs. Quigg.
Bjornstrom, H.
Birnbaum, Jacob.
Blackwell, S. W.
Borebank, J. J.
Bowen, Miss.
Brady, John B.
Brewe, Arthur J.
Butt, Major A.

Clark, Walter M.
Clifford, George Q.
Colley, E. P.
Cardeza, T. D. M., servant of.
Cardeza, Mrs. J. W., maid of.
Carlson, Frank.
Corran, F. M.
Corran, J. P.
Chafee, Mr. H. I.
Chisholm, Robert.
Compton, A. T.
Crafton, John B.
Crosby, Edward G.
Cummings, John Bradley.

Dulles, William C.
Douglas, W. D.
Douglas, Master R., nurse of.

Evans, Miss E.

Fortune, Mark.
Foreman, B. L.
Fortune, Charles.
Franklin, T. P.
Futrelle, J.

Gee, Arthur.
Goldenberg, E. L.
Goldschmidt, G. B.
Giglio, Victor.
Guggenheim, Benjamin.

Hays, Charles M.
Hays, Mrs. Charles, maid of.
Head, Christopher.
Hilliard, H. H.
Hipkins, W. E.
Hogenheim, Mrs. A.
Harris, Henry B.
Harp, Mr. and Mrs. Charles M.
Harp, Miss Margaret, and
    maid.
Holverson, A. M.

Isham, Miss A. E.
Ismay, J. Bruce, servant of.

Julian, H. F.
Jones, C. C.

Kent, Edward A.
Kenyon, Mr. and Mrs. F. R.

ROLL OF THE DEAD—FIRST CABIN (Continued)

Klaber, Herman.

Lamberth, Williams, F. F.
Lawrence, Arthur.
Long, Milton.
Lewy, E. G.
Loring, J. H.
Lingrey, Edward.

Maguire, J. E.
McCaffry, T.
McCaffry, T., Jr.
McCarthy, T.
Middleton, J. C.
Millet, Frank D.
Minahan, Dr.
Meyer, Edgar J.
Molson, H. M.
Moore, C., servant.

Natsch, Charles.
Newall, Miss T.
Nicholson, A. S.

Ovies, S.
Ornout, Alfred T.

Parr, M. H. W.
Pears, Mr. and Mrs. Thomas.
Penasco, Mr. and Mrs. Victor.
Partner, M. A.
Payne, V.
Pond, Florence, and maid.
Porter, Walter.
Puffer, C. C.

Reuchlin, J.
Robert, Mrs. E., maid of.
Roebling, Washington A., 2nd.

Rood, Hugh R.
Roes, J. Hugo.
Rothes, Countess, maid of.
Rothschild, M.
Rowe, Arthur.
Ryerson, A.

Silvey, William B.
Spedden, Mrs. F. O., maid of.
Spencer, W. A.
Stead, W. T.
Stehli, Mr. and Mrs. Max
    Frolicher.
Stone, Mrs. George, maid of.
Straus, Mr. and Mrs. Isidor.
Sutton, Frederick.
Smart, John M.
Smith, Clinch.
Smith. R. W.
Smith, L. P.

Taussig, Emil.
Thayer, Mrs., maid of.
Thayer, John B.
Thorne, G.

Vanderhoof, Wyckoff.

Walker, W. A.
Warren, F. M.
White, Percival, A.
White, Richard F.
Widener, G. D.
Widener, Harry.
Wood, Mr. and Mrs. Frank P.
Weir, J.
Williams, Duane.
Wright, George.

Second Cabin

Abelson, Samson.
Andrew, Frank.
Ashby, John.
Aldworth, C.
Andrew, Edgar.

Bracken, James H.
Brown, Mrs.
Banfield, Fred.
Bright, Narl.
Braily, bandsman.
Breicoux, bandsman.
Bailey, Percy.
Bainbridge, C. R.
Byles, The Rev. Thomas.
Beauchamp, H. J.
Berg, Miss E.
Benthan, I.
Bateman, Robert J.
Butler, Reginald.
Botsford, Hull.
Boweener, Solomon.
Berriman, William.

Clarke, Charles.
Clark, bandsman.
Corey, Mrs. C. P.
Carter, the Rev. Ernest.
Carter, Mrs.
Coleridge, Reginald.
Chapman, Charles.
Cunningham, Alfred.
Campbell, William.
Collyer, Harvey.
Corbett, Mrs. Irene.
Chapman, John H.
Chapman, Mrs. E.
Colander, Eric.
Cotterill, Harry.

Deacon, Percy.
Davis, Charles.
Dibben, William.
De Brito, Jose.
Denborny, H.
Drew, James.
Drew, Master M.
David, Master J. W.
Dounton, W. J.
Del Varlo, S.
Del Varlo, Mrs.

Enander, Ingvar.
Eitemiller, G. F.

Frost, A.
Fynnery, Mr.
Faunthorpe, H.
Fillbrook, C.
Funk, Annie.
Fahlstrom, A.
Fox, Stanley W.

Greenberg, S.
Giles, Ralph.
Gaskell, Alfred.
Gillespie, William.
Gilbert, William.
Gall, S.
Gill, John.
Giles, Edgar.
Giles, Fred.
Gale, Harry.
Gale, Phadruch.
Garvey, Lawrence.

Hickman, Leonard.
Hickman, Lewis.
Hume, bandsman.

ROLL OF THE DEAD—SECOND CABIN (Continued)

Hickman, Stanley.
Hood, Ambrose.
Hodges, Henry P.
Hart, Benjamin.
Harris, Walter.
Harper, John.
Harbeck, W. H.
Hoffman, Mr.
Herman, Mrs. S.
Howard, B.
Howard, Mrs. E. T.
Hale, Reginald.
Hiltunen, M.
Hunt, George.

Jacobson, Mr.
Jacobson, Sydney.
Jeffery, Clifford.
Jeffery, Ernest.
Jenkin, Stephen.
Jarvis, John D.

Keane, Daniel.
Kirkland, Rev. C.
Karnes, Mrs. F. G.
Keynaldo, Miss.
Krillner, J. H.
Krins, bandsman.
Karines, Mrs.
Kantar, Selna.
Knight, R.

Lengam, John.
Levy, R. J.
Lahtiman, William.
Lauch, Charles.
Leyson, R. W. N.
Laroche, Joseph.
Lamb, J. J.

McKane, Peter.
Milling, Jacob.
Mantoila, Joseph.
Malachard, Noll.
Moraweck, Dr.
Mangiovacchi, E.
McCrae, Arthur G.
McCrie, James M.
McKane, Peter D.
Mudd, Thomas.
Mac, Mrs. Mary.
Marshall, Henry.
Mayberg, Frank H.
Meyer, August.
Myles, Thomas.
Mitchell, Henry.
Matthews, W. J.

Nesen, Israel.
Nicholls, Joseph C.
Norman, Robert D.

Otter, Richard.

Phillips, Robert.
Ponesell, Martin.
Pain, Dr. Alfred.
Parkes, Frank.
Pengelly, F.
Pernot, Rene.
Peruschitz, Rev.
Parker, Clifford.
Pulbaum, Frank.

Renouf, Peter H.
Rogers, Harry.
Reeves, David.

Slemen, R. J.

ROLL OF THE DEAD—SECOND CABIN (Continued)

Sobey, Hayden.
Slatter, Miss H. M.
Stanton, Ward.
Sword, Hans K.
Stokes, Philip J.
Sharp, Percival.
Sedgwick, Mr. F. W.
Smith, Augustus.
Sweet, George.
Sjostedt, Ernst.

Taylor, bandsman.
Turpin, William J.
Turpin, Mrs. Dorothy.
Turner, John H.

Turner, John H.
Troupiansky, M.
Tirvan, Mrs. A.

Veale, James.

Watson, E.
Woodward, bandsman.
Ware, William J.
Weisz, Leopold.
Wheadon, Edward.
Ware, John J.
West, E. Arthur.
Wheeler, Edwin.
Werman, Samuel.

The total death list was 1635. Third cabin passengers and crew are not included in the list here given owing to the impossibility of obtaining the exact names of many.

CHAPTER XIII

The Story of Charles F. Hurd

HOW THE TITANIC SANK—WATER STREWN WITH DEAD BODIES—
VICTIMS MET DEATH WITH HYMN ON THEIR LIPS.

THE story of how the Titanic sank is told by Charles F. Hurd, who was a passenger on the Carpathia.

He praised highly the courage of the crew, hundreds of whom gave their lives with a heroism which equaled but could not exceed that of John Jacob Astor, Henry B. Harris, Jacques Futrelle and others in the long list of first-cabin passengers. The account continues:

"The crash against the iceberg, which had been sighted at only a quarter mile distance, came almost simultaneously with the click of the levers operated from the bridge, which stopped the engines and closed the water-tight doors. Captain Smith was on the bridge a moment later, summoning all on board to put on life preservers and ordering the life-boats lowered.

"The first boats had more male passengers, as the men were the first to reach the deck. When the rush of frightened men and women and crying children to the decks began, the 'women first' rule was rigidly enforced.

"Officers drew revolvers, but in most cases there was no use for them. Revolver shots heard shortly before the Titanic went down caused many rumors, one that Captain Smith had shot himself, another that First Officer Murdock had ended his life, but members of the crew discredit these rumors.

"Captain Smith was last seen on the bridge just before the ship sank, leaping only after the decks had been washed away.

"What became of the men with the life-preservers was a question asked by many since the disaster. Many of these with life-preservers were seen to go down despite the preservers, and dead bodies floated on the surface as the boats moved away.

"Facts which I have established by inquiries on the Carpathia, as positively as they could be established in view of the silence of the few surviving officers, are:

"That the Titanic's officers knew, several hours before the crash, of the possible nearness of the icebergs.

"That the Titanic's speed, nearly 23 knots an hour, was not slackened.

"That the number of life-boats on the Titanic was insufficient to accommodate more than one-third of the passengers, to say nothing of the crew. Most members of the crew say there were sixteen life-boats and two collapsibles; none say there were more than twenty boats in all. The 700 escaped filled most of the sixteen life-boats and the one collapsible which got away, to the limit of their capacity.

"Had the ship struck the iceberg head on at whatever speed and with whatever resulting shock, the bulkhead system of water-tight compartments would probably have saved the vessel. As one man expressed it, it was the impossible that happened when, with a shock unbelievably mild, the ship's side was torn for a length which made the bulkhead system ineffective."

After telling of the shock and the lowering of the boats the account continues:

"Some of the boats, crowded too full to give rowers a chance, drifted for a time. Few had provisions or water, there was lack of covering from the icy air, and the only lights were the still undimmed arcs and incandescents of the settling ship, save for one of the first boats. There a steward, who explained to the passengers that he had been shipwrecked twice before, appeared carrying three oranges and a green light.

"That green light, many of the survivors say, was to the shipwrecked hundreds as the pillar of fire by night. Long after the ship had disappeared, and while confusing false lights danced about the boats, the green lantern kept them together on the course which led them to the Carpathia.

"As the end of the Titanic became manifestly but a matter of moments, the oarsmen pulled their boats away, and the chilling waters began to echo splash after splash as passengers and sailors in life-preservers leaped over and started swimming away to escape the expected suction.

"Only the hardiest of constitutions could endure for more than a few moments such a numbing bath. The first vigorous strokes gave way to heart-breaking cries of 'Help! Help!' and stiffened forms were seen floating on the water all around us.

"Led by the green light, under the light of the stars, the boats drew away, and the bow, then the quarter, then the stacks and at last the stern of the marvel-ship of a few days before, passed beneath the waters. The great force of the ship's sinking was unaided by any violence of the elements, and the suction, not so great as had been feared, rocked but mildly the group of boats now a quarter of a mile distant from it.

"Early dawn brought no ship, but not long after 5 A.M. the Carpathia, far out of her path and making eighteen knots, instead of her wonted fifteen, showed her single red and black smokestack upon the horizon. In the joy of that moment, the heaviest griefs were forgotten.

"Soon afterward Captain Rostron and Chief Steward Hughes were welcoming the chilled and bedraggled arrivals over the Carpathia's side.

"Terrible as were the San Francisco, Slocum and Iroquois disasters, they shrink to local events in comparison with this world-catastrophe.

MRS. GEORGE D. WIDENER

Mrs. Widener was saved, but was obliged to leave her husband and son on the sinking ship.

GEORGE D. WIDENER

Who, with his son, was lost. Mr. Widener was a well-known Philadelphia millionaire, son of P. A. B. Widener, traction magnate and financier.

WILLIAM T. STEAD

The great English writer, who was a passenger on board the ill-fated White
Star Line Steamer Titanic.

"True, there were others of greater qualifications and longer experience than I nearer the tragedy—but they, by every token of likelihood, have become a part of the tragedy. The honored must I say the lamented—Stead, the adroit Jacques Futrelle, what might they not tell were their hands able to hold pencil?

"The silence of the Carpathia's engines, the piercing cold, the clamor of many voices in the companionways, caused me to dress hurriedly and awaken my wife, at 5.40 A.M. Monday. Our stewardess, meeting me outside, pointed to a wailing host in the rear dining room and said, 'From the Titanic. She's at the bottom of the ocean.'

"At the ship's side, a moment later, I saw the last of the line of boats discharge their loads, and saw women, some with cheap shawls about their heads, some with the costliest of fur cloaks, ascending the ship's side. And such joy as the first sight of our ship may have given them had disappeared from their faces, and there were tears and signs of faltering as the women were helped up the ladders or hoisted aboard in swings. For lack of room to put them, several of the Titanic's boats, after unloading, were set adrift.

"At our north was a broad ice field, the length of hundreds of Carpathias. Around us on other sides were sharp and glistening peaks. One black berg, seen about 10 A.M., was said to be that which sunk the Titanic."

CHAPTER XIV

THRILLING ACCOUNT BY L. BEASLEY

COLLISION ONLY A SLIGHT JAR—PASSENGERS COULD NOT
BELIEVE THE VESSEL DOOMED—NARROW ESCAPE OF LIFE-
BOATS—PICKED UP BY THE CARPATHIA.

AMONG the most connected and interesting stories related by the survivors was the one told by L. Beasley, of Cambridge, England. He said:

"The voyage from Queenstown had been quite uneventful; very fine weather was experienced, and the sea was quite calm. The wind had been westerly to southwesterly the whole way, but very cold, particularly the last day; in fact after dinner on Saturday evening it was almost too cold to be out on deck at all.

ONLY A SLIGHT JAR

"I had been in my berth for about ten minutes, when, at about 11.15 P.M., I felt a slight jar, and then soon after a second one, but not sufficiently violent to cause any anxiety to anyone, however nervous they may have been. However, the engines stopped immediately afterward, and my first thought was, 'She has lost a propeller.'

"I went up on the top (boat) deck in a dressing gown and found only a few persons there, who had come up similarly to inquire why we had stopped, but there was no sort of anxiety in the minds of anyone.

"We saw through the smoking room window a game of cards going on, and went in to inquire if they knew anything; it seems they felt more of the jar, and, looking through the window, had seen a huge iceberg go by close to the side of the boat. They thought we had just grazed it with a glancing blow, and that the engines had been stopped to see if any damage had been done. No one, of course, had any conception that the vessel had been pierced below by part of the submerged iceberg.

"The game went on without any thought of disaster and I retired to my cabin, to read until we went on again. I never saw any of the players or the onlookers again.

SOME WERE AWAKENED

"A little later, hearing people going upstairs, I went out again and found everyone wanting to know why the engines had stopped. No doubt many were awakened from sleep by the sudden stopping of a vibration to which they had become accustomed during the four days we had been on board. Naturally, with such powerful engines as the Titanic carried, the vibration was very noticeable all the time, and the sudden stopping had something the same effect as the stopping of a loud-ticking grandfather's clock in a room.

"On going on deck again I saw that there was an undoubted list downward from stern to bows, but, knowing nothing of what had happened, concluded some of the front compartments had filled and weighed her down. I went down again to put on warmer clothing, and as I dressed heard an order shouted, 'All passengers on deck with life-belts on.'

"We all walked slowly up, with the belts tied on over our clothing, but even then presumed this was only a wise precaution the captain was taking, and that we should return in a short time and retire to bed.

"There was a total absence of any panic or any expressions of alarm, and I suppose this can be accounted for by the exceedingly calm night and the absence of any signs of the accident.

"The ship was absolutely still, and except for a gentle tilt downward, which I don't think one person in ten would have noticed at that time, no signs of the approaching disaster were visible. She lay just as if she were waiting the order to go on again when some trifling matter had been adjusted.

"But in a few moments we saw the covers lifted from the boats and the crews allotted to them standing by and coiling up the ropes which were to lower them by the pulley blocks into the water.

"We then began to realize it was more serious than had been supposed, and my first thought was to go down and get some more clothing and some money, but, seeing people pouring up the stairs, decided it was better to cause no confusion to people coming up. Presently we heard the order:

" 'All men stand back away from the boats, and all ladies retire to next deck below'—the smoking-room deck or B deck.

MEN STOOD BACK

"The men all stood away and remained in absolute silence leaning against the end railings of the deck or pacing slowly up and down.

"The boats were swung out and lowered from A deck. When they were to the level of B deck, where all the women were collected, they got in quietly, with the exception of some who refused to leave their husbands.

"In some cases they were torn from them and pushed into the boats, but in many instances they were allowed to remain because there was no one to insist they should go.

"Looking over the side, one saw boats from aft already in the water, slipping quietly away into the darkness, and presently the boats near me were lowered, and with much creaking as the new ropes slipped through the pulley blocks down the ninety feet which separated them from the water. An officer in uniform came up as one boat went down and shouted, 'When you are afloat row round to the companion ladder and stand by with the other boats for orders.'

" 'Aye, aye, sir,' came up the reply; but I don't think any boat was able to obey the order. When they were afloat and had the oars at work, the condition of the rapidly settling boat was so much more a sight for alarm for those in the boats than those on board, that in common prudence the sailors saw they could do nothing but row from the sinking ship to save at any rate some lives. They no doubt anticipated that suction from such an enormous vessel would be more dangerous than usual to a crowded boat mostly filled with women.

"All this time there was no trace of any disorder; no panic or rush to the boats and no scenes of women sobbing hysterically, such as one generally pictures as happening at such times— everyone seemed to realize so slowly that there was imminent danger. When it was realized that we might all be presently in the sea with nothing but our life-belts to support us until we were picked up by passing steamers, it was extraordinary how calm everyone was and how completely self-controlled.

"One by one, the boats were filled with women and children, lowered and rowed away into the night. Presently the word went round among the men, 'the men are to be put in boats on the starboard side.'

"I was on the port side, and most of the men walked across the deck to see if this was so. I remained where I was and soon heard the call:

" 'Any more ladies?'

"Looking over the side of the ship, I saw the boat, No. 13, swinging level with B deck, half full of ladies. Again the call was repeated, 'Any more ladies?'

"I saw none come on, and then one of the crew, looking up, said:

" 'Any more ladies on your deck, sir?'

" 'No,' I replied.

" 'Then you had better jump.'

"I dropped in, and fell in the bottom, as they cried 'lower away.' As the boat began to descend two ladies were pushed hurriedly through the crowd on B deck and heaved over into the boat, and a baby of ten months passed down after them. Down we went, the crew calling to those lowering each end to 'keep her level,' until we were some ten feet from the water, and here occurred the only anxious moment we had during the whole of our experience from leaving the deck to reaching the Carpathia.

"Immediately below our boat was the exhaust of the condensers, a huge stream of water pouring all the time from the ship's side just above the water line. It was plain we ought to be quickly away from this, not to be swamped by it when we touched water.

NO OFFICER ABOARD

"We had no officer aboard, nor petty officer or member of the crew to take charge. So one of the stokers shouted: 'Someone find the pin which releases the boat from the ropes and pull it up!' No one knew where it was. We felt on the floor and sides, but found nothing, and it was hard to move among so many people—we had sixty or seventy on board.

"Down we went and presently floated, with our ropes still holding us, the exhaust washing us away from the side of the vessel and the swell of the sea urging us back against the side again. The result of all these forces was an impetus which carried us parallel to the ship's side and directly under boat 14, which had filled rapidly with men and was coming down on us in a way that threatened to submerge our boat.

" 'Stop lowering 14,' our crew shouted, and the crew of No. 14, now only twenty feet above, shouted the same. But the distance to the top was some seventy feet and the creaking pulleys must have deadened all sound to those above, for down she came, fifteen feet, ten feet, five feet and a stoker and I reached up and touched her swinging above our heads. The next drop would have brought her on our heads, but just before she dropped another stoker sprang to the ropes, with his knife.

JUST ESCAPED ANOTHER BOAT

" 'One,' I heard him say, 'two,' as his knife cut through the pulley ropes, and the next moment the exhaust stream had carried us clear, while boat 14 dropped into the water, into the space we had the moment before occupied, our gunwales almost touching.

"We drifted away easily, as the oars were got out, and headed directly away from the ship. The crew seemed to me to be mostly stewards or cooks in white jackets, two to an oar, with a stoker at the tiller. There was a certain amount of shouting from one end of the boat to the other, and discussion as to which way we should go, but finally it was decided to elect the stoker, who was steering, as captain, and for all to obey his orders. He set to work at once to get into touch with the other boats, calling to them and getting as close as seemed wise, so that when the search boats came in the morning to look for us, there would be more chance for all to be rescued by keeping together.

"It was now about 1 A.M.; a beautiful starlight night, with no moon, and so not very light. The sea was as calm as a pond, just a gentle heave as the boat dipped up and down in the swell; an ideal night, except for the bitter cold, for anyone who had to be out in the middle of the Atlantic ocean in an open boat. And if ever there was a time when such a night was needed, surely it was now, with hundreds of people, mostly women and children, afloat hundreds of miles from land.

WATCHED THE TITANIC

"The captain-stoker told us that he had been at sea twenty-six years, and had never yet seen such a calm night on the Atlantic. As we rowed away from the Titanic, we looked back from time to time to watch her, and a more striking spectacle it was not possible for anyone to see.

"In the distance it looked an enormous length, its great bulk outlined in black against the starry sky, every port-hole and saloon blazing with light. It was impossible to think anything could be wrong with such a leviathan, were it not for that ominous tilt downward in the bows, where the water was by now up to the lowest row of port-holes.

"Presently, about 2 A.M., as near as I can remember, we observed it settling very rapidly, with the bows and the bridge completely under water, and concluded it was now only a question of minutes before it went, and so it proved."

Mr. Beasley went on to tell of the spectacle of the sinking of the Titanic, the terrible experiences of the survivors in the lifeboats and their final rescue by the Carpathia as already related.

CHAPTER XV

JACK THAYER'S OWN STORY OF THE WRECK

SEVENTEEN-YEAR-OLD SON OF PENNSYLVANIA RAILROAD OFFICIAL
TELLS MOVING STORY OF HIS RESCUE—TOLD MOTHER TO BE
BRAVE—SEPARATED FROM PARENTS—JUMPED WHEN VESSEL
SANK—DRIFTED ON OVERTURNED BOAT—PICKED UP BY
CARPATHIA.

ONE of the calmest of the passengers was young Jack Thayer, the seventeen-year-old son of Mr. and Mrs. John B. Thayer. When his mother was put into the life-boat he kissed her and told her to be brave, saying that he and his father would be all right. He and Mr. Thayer stood on the deck as the small boat in which Mrs. Thayer was a passenger made off from the side of the Titanic over the smooth sea.

The boy's own account of his experience as told to one of his rescuers is one of the most remarkable of all the wonderful ones that have come from the tremendous catastrophe:

"Father was in bed, and mother and myself were about to get into bed. There was no great shock. I was on my feet at the time and I do not think it was enough to throw anyone down. I put on an overcoat and rushed up on A deck on the port side. I saw nothing there. I then went forward to the bow to see if I could see any signs of ice. The only ice I saw was on the well deck. I could not see very far ahead, having just come out of a brightly lighted room.

"I then went down to our room and my father and mother came on deck with me, to the starboard side of A deck. We could not see anything there. Father thought he saw small pieces of ice floating around, but I could not see any myself. There was no big berg. We walked around to the port side, and the ship had then a fair list to port. We stayed there looking over the side for about five minutes. The list seemed very slowly to be increasing.

"We then went down to our rooms on C deck, all of us dressing quickly, putting on all our clothes. We all put on life-preservers, and over these we put our overcoats. Then we hurried up on deck and walked around, looking out at different places until the women were all ordered to collect on the port side.

SEPARATED FROM PARENTS

"Father and I said good-bye to Mother at the top of the stairs on A deck. She and the maid went right out on A deck on the port side and we went to the starboard side. As at this time we had no idea the boat would sink we walked around A deck and then went to B deck. Then we thought we would go back to see if Mother had gotten off safely, and went to the port side of A deck. We met the chief steward of the main dining saloon and he told us that Mother had not yet taken a boat, and he took us to her.

"Father and Mother went ahead and I followed. They went down to B deck and a crowd got in front of me and I was not able to catch them, and lost sight of them. As soon as I could get through the crowd I tried to find them on B deck, but without success. That is the last time I saw my father. This was about one half an hour before she sank. I then went to the starboard side, thinking that Father and Mother must have gotten off in a boat. All of this time I was with a fellow named Milton C. Long, of New York, whom I had just met that evening.

"On the starboard side the boats were getting away quickly. Some boats were already off in a distance. We thought of getting into one of the boats, the last boat to go on the forward part of

READING ROOM OF THE TITANIC

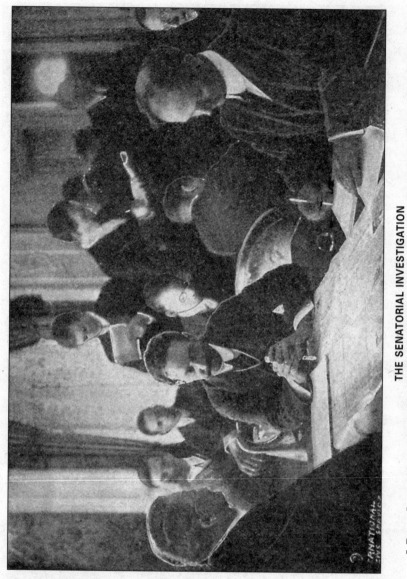

THE SENATORIAL INVESTIGATION

J. Bruce Ismay, Managing Director of the International Mercantile Marine and head of the White Star Line, before the Congressional Investigating Committee, telling how he escaped death when the Titanic foundered.

the starboard side, but there seemed to be such a crowd around I thought it unwise to make any attempt to get into it. He and I stood by the davits of one of the boats that had left. I did not notice anybody that I knew except Mr. Lindley, whom I had also just met that evening. I lost sight of him in a few minutes. Long and I then stood by the rail just a little aft of the captain's bridge.

THOUGHT SHIP WOULD FLOAT

"The list to the port had been growing greater all the time. About this time the people began jumping from the stern. I thought of jumping myself, but was afraid of being stunned on hitting the water. Three times I made up my mind to jump out and slide down the davit ropes and try to make the boats that were lying off from the ship, but each time Long got hold of me and told me to wait a while. He then sat down and I stood up waiting to see what would happen. Even then we thought she might possibly stay afloat.

"I got a sight on a rope between the davits and a star and noticed that she was gradually sinking. About this time she straightened up on an even keel and started to go down fairly fast at an angle of about 30 degrees. As she started to sink we left the davits and went back and stood by the rail about even with the second funnel.

"Long and myself said good-bye to each other and jumped up on the rail. He put his legs over and held on a minute and asked me if I was coming. I told him I would be with him in a minute. He did not jump clear, but slid down the side of the ship. I never saw him again.

"About five seconds after he jumped I jumped out, feet first. I was clear of the ship; went down, and as I came up I was pushed away from the ship by some force. I came up facing the ship, and one of the funnels seemed to be lifted off and fell towards me about 15 yards away, with a mass of sparks and steam coming out of it. I saw the ship in a sort of a red glare, and it seemed to me that she broke in two just in front of the third funnel.

"This time I was sucked down, and as I came up I was pushed out again and twisted around by a large wave, coming up in the midst of a great deal of small wreckage. As I pushed my hand from my head it touched the cork fender of an over-turned life-boat. I looked up and saw some men on the top and asked them to give me a hand. One of them, who was a stoker, helped me up. In a short time the bottom was covered with about twenty-five or thirty men. When I got on this I was facing the ship.

"The stern then seemed to rise in the air and stopped at about an angle of 60 degrees. It seemed to hold there for a time and then with a hissing sound it shot right down out of sight with people jumping from the stern. The stern either pivoted around towards our boat, or we were sucked towards it, and as we only had one oar we couldn't keep away. There did not seem to be very much suction and most of us managed to stay on the bottom of our boat.

"We were then right in the midst of fairly large wreckage, with people swimming all around us. The sea was very calm and we kept the boat pretty steady, but every now and then a wave would wash over it.

SAID THE LORD'S PRAYER

"The assistant wireless operator was right next to me, holding on to me and kneeling in the water. We all sang a hymn and said the Lord's Prayer, and then waited for dawn to come. As often as we saw the other boats in a distance we would yell, 'Ship ahoy!' But they could not distinguish our cries from any of the others, so we all gave it up, thinking it useless. It was very cold and none of us were able to move around to keep warm, the water washing over her almost all the time.

"Toward dawn the wind sprang up, roughening up the water and making it difficult to keep the boat balanced. The wireless man raised our hopes a great deal by telling us that the Carpathia would be up in about three hours. About 3.30 or 4 o'clock some men on our boat on the bow sighted her mast lights. I could not see them, as I was sitting down with a man kneeling on my leg. He finally got up and I stood up. We had the second officer, Mr. Lightoller, on board. We had an officer's whistle and whistled for the boats in the distance to come up and take us off.

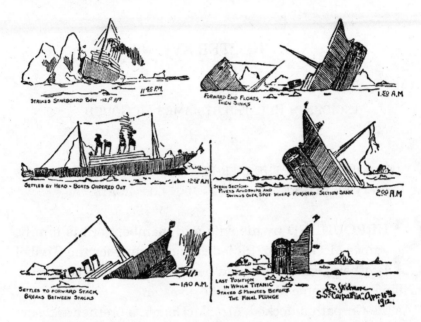

SKETCHES OF THE TITANIC BY "JACK" THAYER
These sketches were outlined by John B. Thayer, Jr., on the day of the disaster, and afterwards filled in by L. D. Skidmon, of Brooklyn.

"It took about an hour and a half for the boats to draw near. Two boats came up. The first took half and the other took the balance, including myself. We had great difficulty about this time in balancing the boat, as the men would lean too far, but we were all taken aboard the already crowded boat, and in about a half or three-quarters of an hour later we were picked up by the Carpathia.

"I have noticed Second Officer Lightoller's statement that 'J. B. Thayer was on our overturned boat,' which would give the impression that it was Father, when he really meant it was I, as he only learned my name in a subsequent conversation on the Carpathia, and did not know I was 'junior'."

CHAPTER XVI

INCIDENTS RELATED BY JAMES MCGOUGH

WOMEN FORCED INTO THE LIFE-BOATS—WHY SOME MEN WERE
SAVED BEFORE WOMEN—ASKED TO MAN LIFE-BOATS.

SURROUNDED by his wife and members of his family,
James McGough, of Philadelphia, a buyer for the Gimbel
Brothers, whose fate had been in doubt, recited a most
thrilling and graphic picture of the disaster.

As the Carpathia docked, Mrs. McGough, a brother and several friends of the buyer, met him, and after the touching reunion
had taken place the party proceeded to Philadelphia.

Vivid in detail, Mr. McGough's story differs essentially from
one the imagination would paint. He declared that the boat was
driving at a high rate of speed at the time of the accident, and
seemed impressed by the calmness and apathy displayed by the
survivors as they tossed on the frozen seas in the little life-boats
until the Carpathia picked them up.

The Titanic did not plunge into the water suddenly, he
declared, but settled slowly into the deep with its hundreds of
passengers.

"The collision occurred at 20 minutes of 12," said Mr. McGough.
"I was sleeping in my cabin when I felt a wrench, not severe or
terrifying.

"It seemed to me to be nothing more serious than the racing

of the screw, which often occurs when a ship plunges her bow deep into a heavy swell, raising the stern out of water. We dressed hurriedly and ran to the upper deck. There was little noise or tumult at the time.

"The promenade deck, being higher from the base of the ship and thus more insecure, strained and creaked; so we went to the lower decks. By this time the engines had been reversed, and I could feel the ship backing off. Officers and stewards ran through the corridors, shouting for all to be calm, that there was no danger. We were warned, however, to dress and put life-preservers on us. I had on what clothing I could find and had stuffed some money in my pocket.

PARTING OF ASTOR AND BRIDE

"As I passed the gymnasium I saw Colonel Astor and his young wife together. She was clinging to him, piteously pleading that he go into the life-boat with her. He refused almost gruffly and was attempting to calm her by saying that all her fears were groundless, that the accident she feared would prove a farce. It proved different, however.

"None, I believe, knew that the ship was about to sink. I did not realize it just then. When I reached the upper deck and saw tons of ice piled upon our crushed bow the full realization came to me.

"Officers stood with drawn guns, ordering the women into the boats. All feared to leave the comparative safety of a broad and firm deck for the precarious smaller boats. Women clung to their husbands, crying that they would never leave without them, and had to be torn away.

"On one point all the women were firm. They would not enter a life-boat until men were in it first. They feared to trust themselves to the seas in them. It required courage to step into the frail crafts as they swung from the creaking davits. Few men were willing to take the chance. An officer rushed behind me and shouted:

" 'You're big enough to pull an oar. Jump into this boat or we'll never be able to get the women off. I was forced to do so, though I admit that the ship looked a great deal safer to me than any small boat.

"Our boat was the second off. Forty or more persons were crowded into it, and with myself and members of the crew at the oars, were pulled slowly away. Huge icebergs, larger than the Pennsylvania depot at New York, surrounded us. As we pulled away we could see boat after boat filled and lowered to the waves. Despite the fact that they were new and supposedly in excellent working order, the blocks jammed in many instances, tilting the boats, loaded with people, at varying angles before they reached the water.

BAND CONTINUED PLAYING

"As the life-boats pulled away the officers ordered the bands to play, and their music did much to quell panic. It was a heart-breaking sight to us, tossing in an eggshell three-fourths of a mile away, to see the great ship go down. First she listed to the star-board, on which side the collision had occurred, then she settled slowly but steadily, without hope of remaining afloat.

"The Titanic was all aglow with lights as if for a function. First we saw the lights of the lower deck snuffed out. A while later and the second deck illumination was extinguished in a similar manner. Then the third and upper decks were darkened, and without plunging or rocking the great ship disappeared slowly from the surface of the sea.

"People were crowded on each deck as it lowered into the water, hoping in vain that aid would come in time. Some of the life-boats caught in the merciless suction were swallowed with her.

"The sea was calm—calm as the water in a tumbler. But it was freezing cold. None had dressed heavily, and all, therefore, suf-fered intensely. The women did not shriek or grow hysterical while we waited through the awful night for help. We men stood at the oars, stood because there was no room for us to sit, and kept the boat headed into the swell to prevent her capsizing. Another boat was at our side, but all the others were scattered around the water.

"Finally, shortly before 6 o'clock, we saw the lights of the Carpathia approaching. Gradually she picked up the survivors in the other boats and then approached us. When we were lifted to the deck the women fell helpless. They were carried to whatever quarters offered themselves, while the men were assigned to he smoking room.

"Of the misery and suffering which was witnessed on the rescue ship I know nothing. With the other men survivors I was glad to remain in the smoking room until New York was reached, trying to forget the awful experience.

"To us aboard the Carpathia came rumors of misstatements which were being made to the public. The details of the wreck were woefully misunderstood.

"Let me emphasize that the night was not foggy or cloudy. There was just the beginning of the new moon, but every star in the sky was shining brightly, unmarred by clouds. The boats were lowered from both sides of the Titanic in time to escape, but there was not enough for all."

CHAPTER XVII

WIRELESS OPERATOR PRAISES HEROIC WORK

STORY OF HAROLD BRIDE, THE SURVIVING WIRELESS OPERATOR OF THE TITANIC, WHO WAS WASHED OVERBOARD AND RESCUED BY LIFE-BOAT—BAND PLAYED RAG-TIME AND "AUTUMN".

ONE of the most connected and detailed accounts of the horrible disaster was that told by Harold Bride, the wireless operator. Mr. Bride said:

"I was standing by Phillips, the chief operator, telling him to go to bed, when the captain put his head in the cabin.

" 'We've struck an iceberg,' the captain said, 'and I'm having an inspection made to tell what it has done for us. You better get ready to send out a call for assistance. But don't send it until I tell you.'

"The captain went away and in ten minutes, I should esti-mate the time, he came back. We could hear a terrific confusion outside, but there was not the least thing to indicate that there was any trouble. The wireless was working perfectly.

" 'Send the call for assistance,' ordered the captain, barely putting his head in the door.

" 'What call shall I send?' Phillips asked.

" 'The regulation international call for help. Just that.'

"Then the captain was gone. Phillips began to send 'C. Q. D.' He flashed away at it and we joked while he did so. All of us made light of the disaster.

"The Carpathia answered our signal. We told her our position and said we were sinking by the head. The operator went to tell the captain, and in five minutes returned and told us that the captain of the Carpathia was putting about and heading for us.

GREAT SCRAMBLE ON DECK

"Our captain had left us at this time and Phillips told me to run and tell him what the Carpathia had answered. I did so, and I went through an awful mass of people to his cabin. The decks were full of scrambling men and women. I saw no fighting, but I heard tell of it.

"I came back and heard Phillips giving the Carpathia fuller directions. Phillips told me to put on my clothes. Until that moment I forgot that I was not dressed.

"I went to my cabin and dressed. I brought an overcoat to Phillips. It was very cold. I slipped the overcoat upon him while he worked.

"Every few minutes Phillips would send me to the captain with little messages. They were merely telling how the Carpathia was coming our way and gave her speed.

"I noticed as I came back from one trip that they were putting off women and children in life-boats. I noticed that the list forward was increasing.

"Phillips told me the wireless was growing weaker. The captain came and told us our engine rooms were taking water and that the dynamos might not last much longer. We sent that word to the Carpathia.

"I went out on deck and looked around. The water was pretty close up to the boat deck. There was a great scramble aft, and how poor Phillips worked through it right to the end I don't know.

"He was a brave man. I learned to love him that night and I suddenly felt for him a great reverence to see him standing there sticking to his work while everybody else was raging about. I will never live to forget the work of Phillips for the last awful fifteen minutes.

"I thought it was about time to look about and see if there was anything detached that would float. I remembered that every member of the crew had a special life-belt and ought to know where it was. I remembered mine was under my bunk. I went and got it. Then I thought how cold the water was.

"I remembered I had an extra jacket and a pair of boots, and I put them on. I saw Phillips standing out there still sending away, giving the Carpathia details of just how we were doing.

"We picked up the Olympia and told her we were sinking by the head and were about all down. As Phillips was sending the message I strapped his life-belt to his back. I had already put on his overcoat. Every minute was precious, so I helped him all I could.

BAND PLAYS IN RAG-TIME

"From aft came the tunes of the band. It was a rag-time tune, I don't know what. Then there was 'Autumn.' Phillips ran aft and that was the last I ever saw of him.

"I went to the place where I had seen a collapsible boat on the boat deck, and to my surprise I saw the boat and the men still trying to push it off. I guess there wasn't a sailor in the crowd. They couldn't do it. I went up to them and was just lending a hand when a large wave came awash of the deck.

"The big wave carried the boat off. I had hold of a row-lock and I went off with it. The next I knew I was in the boat.

"But that was not all. I was in the boat and the boat was upside down and I was under it. And I remember realizing I was wet through, and that whatever happened I must not breathe, for I was under water.

"I knew I had to fight for it and I did. How I got out from under the boat I do not know, but I felt a breath of air at last.

"There were men all around me—hundreds of them. The sea was dotted with them, all depending on their life-belts. I felt I simply had to get away from the ship. She was a beautiful sight then.

"Smoke and sparks were rushing out of her funnel, and there must have been an explosion, but we had heard none. We only saw the big stream of sparks. The ship was gradually turning on her nose—just like a duck does that goes down for a dive. I had one thing on my mind—to get away from the suction. The band was still playing, and I guess they all went down.

"They were playing 'Autumn' then. I swam with all my might. I suppose I was 150 feet away when the Titanic, on her nose, with her after-quarter sticking straight up in the air, began to settle—slowly.

"When at last the waves washed over her rudder there wasn't the least bit of suction I could feel. She must have kept going just as slowly as she had been.

"I forgot to mention that, besides the Olympic and Carpathia, we spoke some German boat, I don't know which, and told them how we were. We also spoke the Baltic. I remembered those things as I began to figure what ships would be coming toward us.

"I felt, after a little while, like sinking. I was very cold. I saw a boat of some kind near me and put all my strength into an effort to swim to it. It was hard work. I was all done when a hand reached out from the boat and pulled me aboard. It was our same collapsible.

"There was just room for me to roll on the edge. I lay there, not caring what happened. Somebody sat on my legs; they were wedged in between slats and were being wrenched. I had not the heart left to ask the man to move. It was a terrible sight all around—men swimming and sinking.

"I lay where I was, letting the man wrench my feet out of shape. Others came near. Nobody gave them a hand. The bottom-up boat already had more men than it would hold and it was sinking.

"At first the larger waves splashed over my head and I had to breathe when I could.

"Some splendid people saved us. They had a right-side-up boat, and it was full to its capacity. Yet they came to us and loaded us all into it. I saw some lights off in the distance and knew a steamship was coming to our aid.

"I didn't care what happened. I just lay, and gasped when I could and felt the pain in my feet. At last the Carpathia was alongside and the people were being taken up a rope ladder. Our boat drew near, and one by one the men were taken off of it.

"The way the band kept playing was a noble thing. I heard it first while we were working wireless, when there was a rag-time tune for us, and the last I saw of the band, when I was floating out in the sea, with my life-belt on, it was on deck playing 'Autumn.' How they ever did it I cannot imagine.

"That and the way Phillips kept sending after the captain told him his life was his own, and to look out for himself, two things that stand out in my mind over all the rest."

CHAPTER XVIII

STORY OF THE STEWARD

PASSENGERS AND CREW DYING WHEN TAKEN ABOARD
CARPATHIA—ONE WOMAN SAVED A DOG—ENGLISH COLONEL
SWAM FOR HOURS WHEN BOAT WITH MOTHER CAPSIZED.

S OME of the most thrilling incidents connected with the rescue of the Titanic's survivors are told in the following accounts given by a man trained to the sea, a steward of the rescue ship Carpathia:

"At midnight on Sunday, April 14th, I was promenading the deck of the steamer Carpathia, bound for the Mediterranean and three days out from New York, when an urgent summons came to my room from the chief steward, E. Harry Hughes. I then learned that the White Star liner Titanic, the greatest ship afloat, had struck an iceberg and was in serious difficulties.

"We were then already steaming at our greatest power to the scene of the disaster, Captain Rostron having immediately given orders that every man of the crew should stand by to exert his utmost efforts. Within a very few minutes every preparation had been made to receive two or three thousand persons. Blankets were placed ready, tables laid with hot soups and coffee, bedding, etc., prepared, and hospital supplies laid out ready to attend to any injured.

"The men were then mustered in the saloon and addressed by the chief steward. He told them of the disaster and appealed to them in a few words to show the world what stuff Britishers were made of, and to add a glorious page to the history of the empire; and right well did the men respond to the appeal. Every life-boat was manned and ready to be launched at a moment's notice. Nothing further could be done but anxiously wait and look out for the ship's distress signal.

"Our Marconi operator, whose unceasing efforts for many hours deserve the greatest possible praise, was unable at this time to get any reply to the urgent inquiries he was sending out, and he feared the worst.

"At last a blue flare was observed, to which we replied with a rocket. Day was just dawning when we observed a boat in the distance.

ICEBERG AND FIRST BOAT SIGHTED

"Eastward on the horizon a huge iceberg, the cause of the disaster, majestically reared two noble peaks to heaven. Rope ladders were already lowered and we hove to near the life-boat, which was now approaching us as rapidly as the nearly exhausted efforts of the men at the oars could bring her.

"Under the command of our chief officer, who worked indefatigably at the noble work of rescue, the survivors in the boat were rapidly but carefully hauled aboard and given into the hands of the medical staff under the organization of Dr. McGee.

"We then learned the terrible news that the gigantic vessel, the unsinkable Titanic, had gone down one hour and ten minutes after striking.

"From this time onward life-boats continued to arrive at frequent intervals. Every man of the Carpathia's crew was unsparing in his efforts to assist, to tenderly comfort each and every survivor. In all, sixteen boatloads were received, containing altogether 720 persons, many in simply their night attire, others in evening dress, as if direct from an after-dinner reception, or

Above: MAIN STAIRWAY ON TITANIC. TOP E DECK

Below: SECOND LANDING. C. DECK. GRAND STAIRWAY

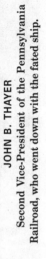

JOHN B. THAYER
Second Vice-President of the Pennsylvania
Railroad, who went down with the fated ship.

MRS. JOHN B. THAYER
Mrs. Thayer and her son were saved. Asked of the disaster, she replied, "It was the most awful thing that anyone could ever conceive."

concert. Most conspicuous was the coolness and self-possession, particularly of the women.

"Pathetic and heartrending incidents were many. There was not a man of the rescue party who was not moved almost to tears. Women arrived and frantically rushed from one gangway to another eagerly scanning the fresh arrivals in the boats for a lost husband or brother.

A CAPSIZED BOAT

"One boat arrived with the unconscious body of an English colonel. He had been taking out his mother on a visit to three others of her sons. He had succeeded in getting her away in one of the boats and he himself had found a place in another. When but a few yards from the ill-fated ship the boat containing his mother capsized before his eyes.

"Immediately he dived into the water and commenced a frantic search for her. But in vain. Boat after boat endeavored to take him aboard, but he refused to give up, continuing to swim for nearly three hours until even his great strength of body and mind gave out and he was hauled unconscious into a passing boat and brought aboard the Carpathia. The doctor gives little hope of his recovery.

"There were, I understand, twelve newly married couples aboard the big ship. The twelve brides have been saved, but of the husbands all but one have perished. That one would not have been here, had he not been urged to assist in manning a life-boat. Think of the self-sacrifice of these eleven heroes, who stood on the doomed vessel and parted from their brides forever, knowing full well that a few brief minutes would end all things for themselves.

"Many similar pathetic incidents could be related. Sad-eyed women roam aimlessly about the ship still looking vainly for husband, brother or father. To comfort them is impossible. All human efforts are being exerted on their behalf. Their material needs are satisfied in every way. But who can cure a broken heart?

SAVED HER POMERANIAN

"One of the earliest boats to arrive was seen to contain a woman tenderly clasping a pet Pomeranian. When assisted to the rope ladder and while the rope was being fastened around her she emphatically refused to give up for a second the dog which was evidently so much to her. He is now receiving as careful and tender attention as his mistress.

"A survivor informs me that there was on the ship a lady who was taking out a huge great Dane dog. When the boats were rapidly filling she appeared on deck with her canine companion and sadly entreated that he should be taken off with her. It was impossible. Human lives, those of women and children, were the first consideration. She was urged to seize the opportunity to save her own life and leave the dog. She refused to desert him and, I understand, sacrificed her life with him.

"One elderly lady was bewailing to a steward that she had lost everything. He indignantly replied that she should thank God her life was spared, never mind her replaceable property. The reply was pathetic:

" 'I have lost everything—my husband,' and she broke into uncontrollable grief.

FOUR BOATS ADRIFT HE SAYS

"One incident that impressed me perhaps more than any other was the burial on Tuesday afternoon of four of the poor fellows who succeeded in safely getting away from the doomed vessel only to perish later from exhaustion and exposure as a result of their gallant efforts to bring to safety the passengers placed in their charge in the life-boats. They were:

"W. H. Hoyte, Esq., first class passenger.

"Abraham Hornner, third class passenger.

"S. C. Siebert, steward.

"P. Lyons, sailor.

"The sailor and steward were unfortunately dead when taken

aboard. The passengers lived but a few minutes after. They were treated with the greatest attention. The funeral service was conducted amid profound silence and attended by a large number of survivors and rescuers. The bodies, covered by the national flag, were reverently consigned to the mighty deep from which they had been, alas, vainly, saved.

"Most gratifying to the officers and men of the Carpathia is the constantly expressive appreciation of the survivors."

He then told of the meeting of the survivors in the cabin of the Carpathia and of the resolution adopted, a statement of which has already been given in another chapter.

CHAPTER XIX

HOW THE WORLD RECEIVED THE NEWS

NATIONS PROSTRATE WITH GRIEF—MESSAGES FROM KINGS
AND CARDINALS—DISASTER STIRS WORLD TO NECESSITY OF
STRICTER REGULATIONS.

YOUNG and old, rich and poor were prostrated by the
news of the disaster. Even Wall Street was neglected. Nor
was the grief confined to America. European nations
felt the horror of the calamity and sent expressions of sympathy.
President Taft made public cablegrams received from the King
and Queen of England, and the King of Belgium, conveying their
sympathy to the American people in the sorrows which have followed the Titanic disaster. The President's responses to both messages were also made public.

The following was the cablegram from King George, dated at
Sandringham:

"The Queen and I are anxious to assure you and the American
nation of the great sorrow which we experienced at the terrible
loss of life that has occurred among the American citizens, as well
as among my own subjects, by the foundering of the Titanic.
Our two countries are so intimately allied by ties of friendship
and brotherhood that any misfortunes which affect the one must
necessarily affect the other, and on the present terrible occasion
they are both equally sufferers.

— "GEORGE R. AND I."

President Taft's reply was as follows:

"In the presence of the appalling disaster to the Titanic the people of the two countries are brought into community of grief through their common bereavement. The American people share in the sorrow of their kinsmen beyond the sea. On behalf of my countrymen I thank you for your sympathetic message.
— "WILLIAM H. TAFT."

The message from King Albert of Belgium was as follows:

"I beg Your Excellency to accept my deepest condolences on the occasion of the frightful catastrophe to the Titanic, which has caused such mourning in the American nation."

The President's acknowledgment follows:

"I deeply appreciate your sympathy with my fellow-country-men who have been stricken with affliction through the disaster to the Titanic."

MESSAGE FROM SPAIN

King Alfonso and Queen Victoria sent the following cablegram to President Taft:

"We have learned with profound grief of the catastrophe to the Titanic, which has plunged the American nation in mourning. We send you our sincerest condolence, and wish to assure you and your nation of the sentiments of friendship and sympathy we feel toward you."

A similar telegram was sent to the King of England.

The many expressions of grief to reach President Taft included one signed jointly by the three American Cardinals, who were in New York attending the meeting of the trustees of the Catholic University. It said:

"To the President of the United States:

"The archbishops of the country, in joint session with the trustees of the Catholic University of America, beg to offer to the President of the United States their expression of their profound grief at the awful loss of human lives attendant upon the sinking of the steamship Titanic, and at the same time to assure the relatives of the victims of this horrible disaster of our deepest sympathy and condolence.

"They wish also to attest hereby to the hope that the lawmakers of the country will see in this sad accident the obvious necessity of legal provisions for greater security of ocean travel.

"James Cardinal Gibbons," *Archbishop of Baltimore.*
"John Cardinal Farley," *Archbishop of New York.*
"William Cardinal O'Connell," *Archbishop of Boston.*

HOUSE ADJOURNED

Formal tribute to the Titanic's dead was paid by the House of Representatives when it adjourned for twenty-four hours.

The prayer of the Rev. Henry N. Couden in opening the House session was, in part:

"We thank Thee that though in the ordinary circumstance of life selfishness and greed seem to be in the ascendancy, yet in times of distress and peril, then it is that the nobility of soul, the Godlike in man, asserts itself and makes heroes."

The flags on the White House and other Government buildings throughout the country were at half-staff.

ROME MOURNED MAJOR BUTT

A special telegram from Rome stated that one of the victims most regretted was Major Butt, whose jovial, bright character made many friends there. Besides autograph letters from the

Pope and Cardinal Merry del Val to President Taft, the major had with him a signed photograph of the Pontiff, given by him personally.

Cardinal Merry del Val had several conversations with Major Butt, who declared that the cardinal was "the first gentleman of Europe." Shortly before he was leaving Rome, regretting that he had not a signed picture of Cardinal Merry del Val, Major Butt entrusted a friend to ask for one. The cardinal willingly put an autograph dedication on a picture recalling their pleasant intercourse.

LONDON NEWSPAPERS CONDEMN LAXITY OF LAW

British indignation, which is not easily excited, was aroused over the knowledge that an antiquated law enabled steamship companies to fail to provide sufficient life-boats to accommodate the passengers and crew of the largest liners in the event of such a disaster as that which occurred to the Titanic. It was insisted that there be an investigation of the loss of life on the Titanic and that the shortage of boats be gone into thoroughly.

The newspapers commented adversely on the lack of boats and their views were emphasized by the knowledge that no attempt has been made to change the regulations in the face of the fact that the inadequacy of boats in such an emergency was called to the attention of Parliament at the time of the collision between the White Star liner Olympia and the cruiser Hawke. It was pointed out at this time that German vessels, much smaller in size than the Olympic, carried more boats and also that these boats were of greater capacity.

T. W. Moore, Secretary of the Merchant Service Guild, when seen at the guild's rooms in Liverpool, said:

"The Titanic disaster is an example, on a colossal scale, of the pernicious and supine system of officials, as represented by the Board of Trade. Modern liners are so designed that they have no accommodations for more life-boats. Among practical seamen it has long been recognized that the modern passenger ship has nothing like adequate boat capacity.

"The Board of Trade has its own views, and the shipowners also have their views, which are largely based upon the economical factor. The naval architects have their opinions, but the practical merchant seaman is not consulted.

"The Titanic disaster is a complete substantiation of the agitation that our guild has carried on for nearly twenty years against the scheme that has precluded practical sea men from being consulted with regard to boat capacity and life-saving appliances.

HOUSE OF COMMONS INVESTIGATION

Immediate and searching inquiry into the Titanic disaster was promised on the floor of the House of Commons April 18th, by President Sidney Buxton, of the Board of Trade, which controls all sea-going vessels.

Buxton, in discussing the utterly inadequate life-saving equipment of the big liner, declared that the committee of the board in charge of life-saving precautions had recently recommended increased life-boats, rafts and life-preservers on all big ships, but that the requirements had been found unsatisfactory and had not been put in force. He frankly admitted the necessity for increased equipment without delay.

The board, he said, was utterly unable to compel the transatlantic vessels to reduce their speed in the contest for "express train" ships. He also said the board could not force ships to take the southerly passage in the spring to avoid ice.

The regulations under which the Titanic carried life-boat accommodations for only about one-third of her passengers and crew had not been revised by the committee since 1894. At that time the regulations were made for ships of "10,000 tons or more." The Titanic's tonnage was 45,000, for which the present requirements are altogether insufficient.

WORK OF RAISING RELIEF FUNDS PROMPT

Several foreign governments telegraphed to the British Government messages of condolence for the sufferers. The King sent a donation of $2625 to the Mansion House fund. Queen Mary donated $1310 and Queen Alexandra $1000 to the same fund.

Oscar Hammerstein proffered, and the lord mayor accepted, the use of his opera house for an entertainment in aid of the fund.

The Shipping Federation donated $10,500 to the Mayor of Southampton's fund, taking care to explain that the White Star Line was not affiliated with the Federation.

Some public institutions also offered to take care of the orphaned children of the crew.

Large firms contributed liberally to the various relief funds, while Covent Garden and other leading theaters prepared special performances to aid in the relief work.

INDIGNANT GERMANY DEMANDS REFORMS

All Germany as well as England was stunned and grieved by the magnitude of the horror of the Titanic catastrophe. Anglo-German recriminations for the moment ceased, as far as the Fatherland was concerned, and profound and sincere compassion for the nation on whom the blow had fallen more heavily was the supreme note of the hour.

The Kaiser, with his characteristic promptitude, was one of the first to communicate his sympathy by telegraph to King George and to the White Star Line. Admiral Prince Henry of Prussia did likewise, and the first act of the Reichstag, after reassembling on Tuesday, was to pass a standing vote of condolence with the British people in their distress.

GERMAN LAWS ALSO INADEQUATE

The German laws, governing the safety appliances on board trans-oceanic vessels, were as archaic and inadequate as those of the British Board of Trade. The maximum provision contained in the German statutes refers to vessels with the capacity of 50,000 cubic metres, which must carry sixteen life-boats. The law also says that if this number of life-boats be insufficient to accommodate all the persons on board, including the crew, there shall be carried elsewhere in the vessel a correspondingly additional number of collapsible life-boats, suitable rafts, floating deckchairs and life-buoys, as well as a generous supply of life-belts.

A vessel of 10,000 tons was a "leviathan" in the days when the German law was passed, and it had undergone no change to meet the conditions, imposed by the construction of vessels twice or three times 10,000 tons, like the Hamburg-American Kaiserin Auguste Victoria, or the North German Lloyd George Washington, to say nothing of the 50,000-ton Imperator, which was added to the Hamburg fleet the next year.

The German lines seemed, like the White Star Company, to have reckoned simply with the practical impossibility of a ship like the Titanic succumbing to the elements.

PERSONAL ANXIETY

Although Germany's and Berlin's direct interest in the passengers aboard the Titanic was less than that of London, New York or Paris, there was the utmost concern for their fate.

Ambassador Leishman and other members of the American Embassy were particularly interested in hearing about Major "Archie" Butt, who passed through Berlin, less than a month before the disaster, en route from Russia and the Far East. Vicepresident John B. Thayer and family, of Philadelphia, were also in Berlin a fortnight earlier and were guests of the American Consul General and Mrs. Thackara. A score of other lesser known passengers had recently stayed in Berlin hotels, and it was local friends or kinsmen of theirs who were in a state of distressing unrest over their fate.

Their anxiety was aggravated by the old-fogey methods of the German newspapers, which were invariably twelve or fifteen hours later than journals, elsewhere in Europe on world news events. Although New York, London and Paris had the cruel truth with their morning papers on Tuesday, it was not until the middle of the forenoon that "extras" made the facts public in Berlin.

William T. Stead was well and favorably known in Germany, and his fate was keenly and particularly mourned. Germans also noted that many Americans of direct Teutonic ancestry or origin were among the shining marks in the death list. Colonel John Jacob Astor was claimed as of German extraction, as well as Isidor Straus, Benjamin Guggenheim, Washington Roebling and Henry B. Harris. All of them had been in Germany frequently and had a wide circle of friends and acquaintances.

Only one well-known resident of Berlin was aboard the Titanic, Far Antoine, whose name appears among the rescued.

CHAPTER XX

BRAVERY OF THE OFFICERS AND CREW

ILLUSTRIOUS CAREER OF CAPTAIN E. J. SMITH—BRAVE TO THE LAST—MAINTENANCE OF ORDER AND DISCIPLINE—ACTS OF HEROISM—ENGINEERS DIED AT POSTS—NOBLE-HEARTED BAND.

IN the anxious hours of uncertainty, when the air cracked and flashed with the story of disaster, there was never doubt in the minds of men ashore about the master of the Titanic. Captain Smith would bring his ship into port if human power could mend the damage the sea had wrought, or if human power could not stay the disaster he would never come to port. There is something Calvinistic about such men of the old-sea breed. They go down with their ships, of their own choice.

Into the last life-boat that was launched from the ship Captain Smith with his own hand lifted a small child into a seat beside its mother. As the gallant officer performed his simple act of humanity several who were already on the boat tried to force the captain to join them, but he turned away resolutely toward the bridge.

That act was significant. Courteous, kindly, of quiet demeanor and soft words, he was known and loved by thousands of travelers.

When the English firm, A. Gibson & Co., of Liverpool, purchased the American clipper, Senator Weber, in 1869, Captain

Smith, then a boy, sailed on her. For seven years he was an apprentice on the Senator Weber, leaving that vessel to go to the Lizzie Fennell, a square rigger, as fourth officer. From there he went to the old Celtic of the White Star Line as fourth officer and in 1887 he became captain of that vessel. For a time he was in command of the freighters Cufic and Runic; then he became skipper of the old Adriatic. Subsequently he assumed command of the Celtic, Britannic, Coptic (which was in the Australian trade), Germanic, Baltic, Majestic, Olympic and Titanic, an illustrious list of vessels for one man to have commanded during his career.

It was not easy to get Captain Smith to talk of his experiences. He had grown up in the service, was his comment, and it meant little to him that he had been transferred from a small vessel to a big ship and then to a bigger ship and finally to the biggest of them all.

"One might think that a captain taken from a small ship and put on a big one might feel the transition," he once said. "Not at all. The skippers of the big vessels have grown up to them, year after year, through all these years. First there was the sailing vessel and then what we would now call small ships—they were big in the days gone by—and finally the giants to-day."

DISASTER TO OLYMPIC

Only once during all his long years of service was he in trouble, when the Olympic, of which he was in command, was rammed by the British cruiser Hawke in the Solent on September 20, 1911. The Hawke came steaming out of Portsmouth and drew alongside the giantess. According to some of the passengers on the Olympic the Hawke swerved in the direction of the big liner and a moment later the bow of the Hawke was crunching steel plates in the starboard quarter of the Olympic, making a thirty-foot hole in her. She was several months in dry dock.

The result of a naval court inquiry was to put all the blame for the collision on the Olympic. Captain Smith, in his testimony before the naval courts said that he was on the bridge when he saw the Hawke overhauling him. The Olympic began to draw ahead later or the Hawke drop astern, the captain did not know which. Then the cruiser turned very swiftly and struck the Olympic at right angles on the quarter. The pilot gave the signal for the Olympic to port, which was to minimize the force of the collision. The Olympic's engines had been stopped by order of the pilot.

Up to the moment the Hawke swerved, Captain Smith said, he had no anxiety. The pilot, Bowyer, corroborated the testimony of Captain Smith. That the line did not believe Captain Smith was at fault, notwithstanding the verdict of the board of naval inquiry, was shown by his retention as the admiral of the White Star fleet and by his being given the command of the Titanic.

Up to the time of the collision with the Hawke Captain Smith when asked by interviewers to describe his experiences at sea would say one word, "uneventful." Then he would add with a smile and a twinkle of his eyes:

"Of course there have been winter gales and storms and fog and the like in the forty years I have been on the seas, but I have never been in an accident worth speaking of. In all my years at sea I have seen but one vessel in distress. That was a brig the crew of which was taken off in a boat by my third officer. I never saw a wreck. I never have been wrecked. I have never been in a predicament that threatened to end in disaster of any sort."

THE CAPTAIN'S LOVE OF THE SEA

Once the interviewer stopped asking personal questions, Captain Smith would talk of the sea, of his love for it, how its appeal to him as a boy had never died.

"The love of the ocean that took me to sea as a boy has never died," he once said. "When I see a vessel plunging up and down in the trough of the sea, fighting her way through and over great waves, and keeping her keel and going on and on—the wonder of the thing fills me, how she can keep afloat and get safely to

VESSEL WITH BOTTOM OF HULL RIPPED OPEN

A view of the torpedo destroyer Tiger, taken in drydock after her collision with the Portland Breakwater in September, 1911; the damage to the Tiger, which is plainly shown in the photograph, is of the same character, though on a smaller scale, as that which was done to the Titanic.

A VIEW OF THE OLYMPIC

The sister-ship of the Titanic, showing the damage done to her hull in the collision with British war vessel, Hawke, in the British Channel.

port? I have never outgrown the wild grandeur of the sea."

When he was in command of the Adriatic, which was built before the Olympic, Captain Smith said he did not believe a disaster with loss of life could happen to the Adriatic.

"I cannot conceive of any vital disaster happening to the Adriatic," he said. "Modern shipbuilding has gone beyond that. There will be bigger boats The depth of harbors seems to be the great drawback at present. I cannot say, of course, just what the limit will be, but the larger boat will surely come. But speed will not develop with size, so far as merchantmen are concerned.

"The traveling public prefers the large comfortable boat of average speed, and anyway that is the boat that pays. High speed eats up money mile by mile, and extreme high speed is suicidal. There will be high speed boats for use as transports and a wise government will assist steamship companies in paying for them, as the English Government is now doing in the cases of the Lusitania and Mauretania, twenty-five knot boats; but no steamship company will put them out merely as a commercial venture."

Captain Smith believed the Titanic to be unsinkable.

BRAVE TO THE LAST

And though the ship turned out to be sinkable, the captain, by many acts of bravery in the face of death, proved that his courage was equal to any test.

Captain Inman Sealby, commander of the steamer Republic, which was the first vessel to use the wireless telegraph to save her passengers in a collision, spoke highly of the commander of the wrecked Titanic, calling him one of the ablest seamen in the world.

"I am sure that Captain Smith did everything in his power to save his passengers. The disaster is one about which he could have had no warning. Things may happen at sea that give no warning to ships' crews and commanders until the harm comes. I believe from what I read that the Titanic hit an iceberg and glanced off, but that the berg struck her from the bottom and tore a great hole."

Many survivors have mentioned the captain's name and narrated some incident to bring out his courage and helpfulness in the emergency; but it was left to a fireman on board the Titanic to tell the story of his death and to record his last message. This man had gone down with the White Star giantess and was clinging to a piece of wreckage for about half an hour before he finally joined several members of the Titanic's company on the bottom of a boat which was floating about among other wreckage near the Titanic.

Harry Senior, the fireman, with his eight or nine companions in distress, had just managed to get a firm hold in the upturned boat when they saw the Titanic rearing preparatory to her final plunge. At that moment, according to the fireman's story, Captain Smith jumped into the sea from the promenade deck of the Titanic with a little girl clutched in his arms. It took only a few strokes to bring him to the upturned boat, where a dozen hands were stretched out to take the little child from his arms and drag him to a point of safety.

"Captain Smith was dragged onto the upturned boat," said the fireman. "He had a life-buoy and a life-preserver. He clung there for a moment and then he slid off again. For a second time he was dragged from the icy water. Then he took off his life-preserver, tossed the life-buoy on the inky waters, and slipped into the water again with the words: "I will follow the ship.""

OTHER FAITHFUL MEN

Nor was the captain the only faithful man on the ship. Of the many stories told by survivors all seem to agree that both officers and crew behaved with the utmost gallantry and that they stuck by the ship nobly to the last.

"Immediately after the Titanic struck the iceberg," said one of the survivors, "the officers were all over the ship reassuring the passengers and calming the more excitable. They said there was no cause for alarm. When everything was quieted they told us we might go back to bed, as the ship was safe. There was no confusion and many returned to their beds.

"We did not know that the ship was in danger until a comparatively short time before she sank. Then we were called on deck and the life-boats were filled and lowered.

"The behavior of the ship's officers at this time was wonderful. There was no panic, no scramble for places in the boats." Later there was confusion, and according to most of the passengers' narratives, there were more than fifty shots fired upon the deck by officers or others in the effort to maintain the discipline.

FIFTH OFFICER LOWE

A young English woman who requested that her name be omitted told a thrilling story of her experience in one of the collapsible boats which had been manned by eight of the crew from the Titanic. The boat was in command of the fifth officer, H. Lowe, whose actions she described as saving the lives of many people. Before the life-boat was launched he passed along the port deck of the steamer, commanding the people not to jump in the boats, and otherwise restraining them from swamping the craft. When the collapsible was launched Officer Lowe succeeded in putting up a mast and a small sail. He collected the other boats together; in some cases the boats were short of adequate crews, and he directed an exchange by which each was adequately manned. He threw lines connecting the boats together, two by two, and thus all moved together. Later on he went back to the wreck with the crew of one of the boats and succeeded in picking up some of those who had jumped overboard and were swimming about. On his way back to the Carpathia he passed one of the collapsible boats which was on the point of sinking with thirty passengers aboard, most of them in scant night-clothing. They were rescued just in the nick of time.

ENGINEERS DIED AT POSTS

There were brave men below deck, too. "A lot has been printed in the papers about the heroism of the officers," said one survivor, "but little has been said of the bravery of the men below decks. I was told that seventeen enginemen who were drowned side by side got down on their knees on the platform of the engine room and prayed until the water surged up to their necks. Then they stood up, clasped hands so as to form a circle and died together. All of these men helped rake the fires out from ten of the forward boilers after the crash. This delayed the explosion and undoubtedly permitted the ship to remain afloat nearly an hour longer, and thus saved hundreds of lives."

In the list of heroes who went down on the Titanic the names of her engineers will have a high place, for not a single engineer was saved. Many of them, no doubt, could not get to the deck, but they had equally as good a chance as the firemen, sixty-nine of whom were saved.

The supposition of those who manned the Titanic was that the engineers, working below, were the first to know the desperate character of the Titanic's injury. The watch called the others, and from that time until the vessel was ready for her last plunge they were too hard at work to note more than that there was a constant rise of water in the hull, and that the pumps were useless.

It was engineers who kept the lights going, saw to the proper closing of bulkhead doors and kept the stoke hole at work until the uselessness of the task was apparent. Most of them probably died at their post of duty.

The Titanic carried a force of about sixty engineers, and in addition she had at least twenty-five "guarantee" engineers, representatives of Harland and Wolff, the builders, and those who had the contract for the engineering work. This supplementary force was under Archie Frost, the builders' chief engineer, and the regular force was under Chief Engineer William Bell, of the White Star Line.

On the line's ships there is the chief engineer, senior and junior second, senior and junior third, and senior and junior fourth engineers. The men are assigned each to his own task. There are hydraulic, electric, pump and steam packing men, and the "guarantee" engineers, representing the builders and the contractors.

The duty of the "guarantee" engineers is to watch the working of the great engines and to see that they are tuned up and in working order. They also watch the working of each part of the machinery which had nothing to do with the actual speed of the ship, principally the electric light dynamos and the refrigerating plant.

NOBLE-HEARTED BAND

"But what of the bandsmen? Who were they?"

This question was asked again and again by all who read the story of the Titanic's sinking and of how the brave musicians played to the last, keeping up the courage of those who were obliged to go down with the ship.

Many efforts were made to find out who the men were, but little was made public until the members of the orchestra of the steamship Celtic reached shore for the first time after the disaster. One of their first queries was about the musicians of the Titanic. Their anxiety was greater than that of any New Yorker, for the members of the band of the Celtic knew intimately the musicians of the ill-fated liner.

"Not one of them saved!" cried John S. Carr, 'cellist on the Celtic. "It doesn't seem possible they have all gone.

"We knew most of them well. They were Englishmen, you know—every one of them, I think. Nearly all the steamship companies hire their musicians abroad, and the men interchange between the ships frequently, so we get a chance to know one another pretty well. The musicians for the Titanic were levied from a number of other White Star ships, but most of the men who went down with the Titanic had bunked with us at some time."

"The thing I can't realize is that happy 'Jock' Hume is dead," exclaimed Louis Cross, a player of the bass viol. "He was the merriest, happiest young Scotchman you ever saw. His family have been making musical instruments in Scotland for generations. I heard him say once that they were minstrels in the old days. It is certainly hard to believe that he is not alive and having his fun somewhere in the world."

At least he helped to make the deaths of many less cruel.

CHAPTER XXI

SEARCHING FOR THE DEAD

SENDING OUT THE MACKAY-BENNETT AND MINIA—BREMEN
PASSENGERS SEE BODIES—IDENTIFYING BODIES—CONFUSION
IN NAMES—RECOVERIES.

A FEW days after the disaster the cable steamer Mackay-Bennett was sent out by the White Star Line to cruise in the vicinity of the disaster and search for missing bodies. Two wireless messages addressed to J. Bruce Ismay, president of the International Mercantile Marine Company, were received on April 21st at the offices of the White Star Line from the cable ship Mackay-Bennett, via Cape Race, one of which reported that the steamship Rhein had sighted bodies near the scene of the Titanic wreck. The first message, which was dated April 20th, read:

"Steamer Rhein reports passing wreckage and bodies 42.1 north, 49.13 west, eight miles west of three big icebergs. Now making for that position. Expect to arrive 8 o'clock to-night.

(Signed)   — "MACKAY-BENNETT"

The second message read:

"Received further information from Bremen [presumably steamship Bremen] and arrived on ground at 8 o'clock P. M. Start

on operation to-morrow. Have been considerably delayed on passage by dense fog.

(Signed)   — "MACKAY-BENNETT"

After receiving these messages Mr. Ismay issued the following statement:

"The cable ship Mackay-Bennett has been chartered by the
White Star Line and ordered to proceed to the scene of the
disaster and do all she could to recover the bodies and glean all
information possible.

"Every effort will be made to identify bodies recovered, and
any news will be sent through immediately by wireless. In addition to any such message as these, the Mackay-Bennett will make
a report of its activities each morning by wireless, and such
reports will be made public at the offices of the White Star Line.

"The cable ship has orders to remain on the scene of the wreck
for at least a week, but should a large number of bodies be recovered before that time she will return to Halifax with them. The
search for bodies will not be abandoned until not a vestige of hope
remains for any more recoveries.

"The Mackay-Bennett will not make any soundings, as they
would not serve any useful purpose, because the depth where the
Titanic sank is more than 2000 fathoms."

On April 22d the first list of twenty-seven names of bodies
recovered was made public. It contained that of Frederick Sutton,
a well-known member of the Union League of Philadelphia. It
did not contain the name of any other prominent man who perished, although it was thought that the name "George W. Widen"
might refer to George D. Widener, son of P. A. B. Widener, of
Philadelphia. The original passenger lists of the Titanic did not
mention "Widen," which apparently established the identity of
the body as that of Mr. Widener, who, together with his son,
Harry, was lost.

The wireless message, after listing the names, concluded, "All
preserved," presumably referring to the condition of the bodies.

A number of the names in the list did not check up with the Titanic's passenger list, which led to the belief that a number of the bodies recovered were members of the Titanic's crew.

MINIA SENT TO ASSIST

At noon, April 23d, there was posted on the bulletin in the White Star office this message from the Mackay-Bennett dated Sunday, April 21st:

"Latitude, 41.58; longitude, 49.21. Heavy southwest swell has interfered with operations. Seventy-seven bodies recovered. All not embalmed will be buried at sea at 8 o'clock to-night with divine service. Can bring only embalmed bodies to port."

To Captain Lardner, master of the Mackay-Bennett, P. A. S. Franklin, vice-president of the White Star Line, sent an urgent message asking that the company be advised at once of all particulars concerning the bodies identified, and also given any information that might lead to the identification of others. He said it was very important that every effort be made to bring all of the bodies possible to port.

Mr. Franklin then directed A. G. Jones, the Halifax agent of the White Star Line, to charter the Minia and send her to the assistance of the Mackay-Bennett. Mr. Jones answered this telegram, and said that the Minia was ready to proceed to sea, but that a southeast gale, which generally brings fog, might delay her departure. She left for Halifax.

NAMES BADLY GARBLED

On April 24th no wireless message was received from the Mackay-Bennett, but the White Star Line officials and telegraphers familiar with the wireless alphabet were busy trying to reconcile some of the names received with those of persons who went down on the Titanic. That the body of William T. Stead, the English journalist and author, had been recovered by the Mackay-Bennett, but through a freakish error in wireless transmission the name of another was reported instead, was one of the theories advanced by persons familiar with the Morse code.

BREMEN SIGHTED MORE THAN A HUNDRED BODIES

When the German liner Bremen reached New York the account of its having sighted bodies of the Titanic victims was obtained.

From the bridge, officers of the ship saw more than a hundred bodies floating on the sea, a boat upside down, together with a number of small pieces of wood, steamer chairs and other wreckage. As the cable ship Mackay-Bennett was in sight, and having word that her mission was to look for bodies, no attempt was made by the Bremen's crew to pick up the corpses.

In the vicinity was seen an iceberg which answered the description of the one the Titanic struck. Smaller bergs were sighted the same day, but at some distance from where the Titanic sank.

The officers of the Bremen did not care to talk about the tragic spectacle, but among the passengers several were found who gave accounts of the dismal panorama through which their ship steamed.

Mrs. Johanna Stunke, a first-cabin passenger, described the scene from the liner's rail.

"It was between 4 and 5 o'clock, Saturday, April 20th," she said, "when our ship sighted an iceberg off the bow to the starboard. As we drew nearer, and could make out small dots floating around in the sea, a feeling of awe and sadness crept over everyone on the ship.

"We passed within a hundred feet of the southernmost drift of the wreckage, and looking down over the rail we distinctly saw a number of bodies so clearly that we could make out what they were wearing and whether they were men or women.

ISIDOR STRAUS

The New York millionaire merchant and philanthropist who lost his life when
the giant Titanic foundered at sea after hitting an iceberg.

ICEBERG PHOTOGRAPHED NEAR SCENE OF DISASTER

This photograph shows what is quite probably the identical iceberg with which the Titanic collided, being taken from the freight steamer Eutonia, less than two days before the accident to the Titanic, in latitude 42° N. and longitude 49.50° W. The disaster occurred in latitude 41.46° N. and longitude 50.14° W, or where the iceberg might easily have turned by the time the Titanic approached this spot.

"We saw one woman in her night dress, with a baby clasped closely to her breast. Several women passengers screamed and left the rail in a fainting condition. There was another woman, fully dressed, with her arms tight around the body of a shaggy dog.

"The bodies of three men in a group, all clinging to one steamship chair, floated near by, and just beyond them were a dozen bodies of men, all of them encased in life-preservers, clinging together as though in a last desperate struggle for life. We couldn't see, but imagined that under them was some bit of wreckage to which they all clung when the ship went down, and which didn't have buoyancy enough to support them.

"Those were the only bodies we passed near enough to distinguish, but we could see the white life-preservers of many more dotting the sea, all the way to the iceberg. The officers told us that was probably the berg hit by the Titanic, and that the bodies and ice had drifted along together."

Mrs. Stunke said a number of the passengers demanded that the Bremen stop and pick up the bodies, but the officers assured them that they had just received a wireless message saying the cable ship Mackay-Bennett was only two hours away from the spot, and was coming for that express purpose.

Other passengers corroborated Mrs. Stunke.

THE IDENTIFIED DEAD

On April 25th the White Star Line officials issued a corrected list of the identified dead. While the corrected list cleared up two or more of the wireless confusions that caused so much speculation in the original list, there still remained a few names that so far as the record of the Titanic showed were not on board that ship when she foundered.

The new list, however, established the fact that the body of George D. Widener, of Philadelphia, was among those on the Mackay-Bennett, and two of the bodies were identified as those of men named Butt.

THE MACKAY-BENNETT RETURNS TO PORT

After completing her search the Mackay-Bennett steamed for Halifax, reaching that port on Tuesday, April 30th. With her flag at half mast, the death ship docked slowly. Her crew manned the rails with bared heads, and on the aft deck were stacked the caskets with the dead. The vessel carried on board 190 bodies, and announcement was made that 113 other bodies had been buried at sea.

Everybody picked up had been in a life-belt and there were no bullet holes in any. Among those brought to port were the bodies of two women.

THE MINIA GIVES UP THE SEARCH

When at last the Minia turned her bow toward shore only thirteen additional bodies had been recovered, making a total of 316 bodies found by the two ships.

Further search seemed futile. Not only had the two vessels gone thoroughly over as wide a field as might likely prove fruitful, but, in addition, the time elapsed made it improbable that other bodies, if found, could be brought to shore. Thus did the waves completely enforce the payment of their terrible toll.

LIST OF IDENTIFIED DEAD

Following is a list of those whose identity was wholly or partially established:

Astor, John Jacob.	Anderson, W. Y.
Adonis, J.	Allison, H. J.
Ale, William.	
Artagaveytia, Ramon.	Butt, W. (seaman).
Ashe, H. W.	Butt, W. (may be Major Butt).
Adahl, Mauritz.	Butterworth, Abelj.
Anderson, Thomas.	Bailey, G. F.
Adams, J.	Barker, E. T.
Aspalande, Carl.	Butler, Reginald.
Allen, H.	Birnbaum, Jacob.

Bristow, R. C.
Buckley, Katherine.

Chapman, John H.
Chapman, Charles.
Connors, P.
Clong, Milton.
Cox, Denton.
Cavendish, Tyrrell W.
Carbines, W.

Dutton, F.
Dashwood, William.
Dulles, W. C.
Douglas, W. D.
Drazenoui, Yosip (referring
probably to Joseph Draznovic).
Donati, Italo (waiter).

Engineer, A. H. F.
Elliott, Edward.

Farrell, James.
Faunthorpe, H.

Gill, J. H.
Greenberg, H.
Gilinski, Leslie.
Graham, George.
Giles, Ralph.
Givard, Hans C.

Hansen, Henry D.
Haytor, A.
Hays, Charles M.
Hodges, H. P.
Hell, J. C.
Hewitt, T.
Harrison, H. H.
Hale, Reg.

Hendekeric, Toznai.
Hinton, W.
Harbeck, W. H.
Holverdon, A. O. (probably A. M.
Halverson of Troy).
Hoffman, Louis M.
Hinckley, G.
Hospital Attendant, no
name given.

Johansen, Malcolm.
Johansen, Eric.
Johansson, Gustaf J.
Johansen, A. F.
Jones, C. C.

Kelly, James.

Laurence, A.
Louch, Charles.
Long, Milton C.
Lilly, A.
Linhart, Wenzell.
Marriortt, W. H. (no such name
appears on the list of
passengers or crew).
Mangin, Mary.
McNamee, Mrs. N. (prob-
ably Miss Elleen McNamee).
Mack, Mrs.
Monros, Jean.
McCaffry, Thomas.
Morgan, Thomas.
Moen, Segurd H.

Newell, T. H.
Nasser, Nicolas.
Norman, Robert D.

Petty, Edwin H.
Partner, Austin.

Penny, Olsen F.
Poggi, ———.

Ragozzi, A. Boothby.
Rice, J. R.
Robins, A.
Robinson, J. M.
Rosenshine, George.

Stone, J.
Steward, 76.
Stokes, Philip J.
Stanton, W.
Straus, Isidor.
Sage, William.
Shea, ———.
Sutton, Frederick.
Sother, Simon.
Schedid, Nihil.
Swane, George.
Sebastiano, Del Carlo.
Stanbrocke, A.

Tomlin, Etnest P.
Talbot, G.

Villner, Hendrick D.
Vassilios, Catalevas (thought
    to be a confusion of two
    surnames).
Vear, W. (may be W. J. Ware
    or W. T. Stead).

Widener, George W.
Williams, Leslie.
Wirz, Albert.
Wiklund, Jacob A.
Wailens, Achille.
White, F. F.
Woody, O. S.
Wersz, Leopold.

Zacarian, Mauri Der

CHAPTER XXII

CRITICISM OF ISMAY

CRIMINAL AND COWARDLY CONDUCT CHARGED—PROPER CAUTION
NOT EXERCISED WHEN PRESENCE OF ICEBERGS WAS KNOWN—
SHOULD HAVE STAYED ON BOARD TO HELP IN WORK OF RESCUE—
SELFISH AND UNSYMPATHETIC ACTIONS ON BOARD THE CAR-
PATHIA—ISMAY'S DEFENSE—WILLIAM E. CARTER'S STATEMENT.

FROM the moment that Bruce Ismay's name was seen
among those of the survivors of the Titanic he became
the object of acrid attacks in every quarter where the
subject of the disaster was discussed. Bitter criticism held that
he should have been the last to leave the doomed vessel.

His critics insisted that as managing director of the White Star
Line his responsibility was greater even than Captain Smith's,
and while granting that his survival might still be explained,
they condemned his apparent lack of heroism. Even in England
his survival was held to be the one great blot on an otherwise
noble display of masculine courage.

A prominent official of the White Star Line shook his head
meaningfully when asked what he thought of Ismay's escape with
the women and children: The general feeling seemed to be that
he should have stayed aboard the sinking vessel, looking out for
those who were left, playing the man like Major Butt and many
another and going down with the ship like Captain Smith.

He was also charged with urging a speed record and with ignoring information received with regard to icebergs.

FEELING IN ENGLAND

The belief in England was that the captain of the Carpathia had acted under Ismay's influence in refusing to permit any account of the disaster to be transmitted previous to the arrival of the vessel in New York. Ismay's telegram making arrangements for the immediate deportation of the survivors among the Titanic's crew was taken to be part of the same scheme to delay if not to prevent their stories of the wreck from being obtained in New York.

Another circumstance which created a damaging impression was Ismay's failure to give the names of the surviving crew, whose distraught families were entitled to as much consideration as those whose relatives occupied the most expensive suites on the Titanic. The anguish endured by the families of members of the crew was reported as indescribable, and Southampton was literally turned into a city of weeping and tragic pathos. The wives of two members of the crew died of shock and suspense.

CRIED FOR FOOD

Mr. Ismay's actions while on the Carpathia were also criticised as selfish and unwarrantable.

"For God's sake get me something to eat, I'm starved. I don't care what it costs or what it is. Bring it to me."

This was the first statement made by Mr. Ismay a few minutes after he was landed on the Carpathia. It is vouched for by an officer of the Carpathia who requested that his name be withheld. This officer gave one of the most complete stories of the events that took place on the Carpathia from the time she received the Titanic's appeal for assistance until she landed the survivors at the Cunard Line pier.

"Ismay reached the Carpathia in about the seventh lifeboat," said the officer. " I didn't know who he was, but afterward I heard the other members of the crew discussing his desire to get something to eat the minute he put his foot on deck. The steward who waited on him reported that Ismay came dashing into the dining room and said:

" 'Hurry, for God's sake, and get me something to eat, I'm starved. I don't care what it costs or what it is. Bring it to me.'"

"The steward brought Ismay a load of stuff and when he had finished it he handed the man a two dollar bill. 'Your money is no good on this ship,' the steward told him.

" 'Take it,' insisted Ismay. 'I am well able to afford it. I will see to it that the boys of the Carpathia are well rewarded for this night's work.'

"This promise started the steward making inquiries as to the identity of the man he had waited on. Then we learned that he was Ismay. I did not see Ismay after the first few hours. He must have kept to his cabin."

REPLY TO CHARGES

Mr. Ismay's plans had been to return immediately to England, and he had wired that the steamer Cedric be held for himself and officers and members of the crew; but public sentiment and subpoenas of the Senate's investigating committee prevented. In the face of the criticism aimed against him, Mr. Ismay issued a long statement in which he not only disclaimed responsibility for the Titanic's fatal collision, but also sought to clear himself of blame for everything that happened after the big ship was wrecked.

He laid the responsibility for the tragedy on Captain Smith. He expressed astonishment that his own conduct in the disaster had been made the subject of inquiry. He denied that he gave any order to Captain Smith. His position aboard was that of any other first cabin passenger, he insisted, and he was never consulted by the captain. He denied telling anyone that he wished the ship to make a speed record. He called attention to the routine

clause in the instructions to White Star captains ordering them
to think of safety at all times. He did not dine with the captain,
he said, and when the ship struck the berg, he was not sitting
with the captain in the saloon.

The managing director added that he was in his stateroom
when the collision occurred. He told of helping to send women
and children away in life-boats on the starboard side, and said
there was no woman in sight on deck when he and William E.
Carter, of Bryn Mawr, Pa., entered the collapsible boat—the
last small craft left on that side of the vessel. He asserted that
he pulled an oar and denied that in sending the three messages
from the Carpathia, urging the White Star officials to hold the
Cedric for the survivors of the Titanic's officers and crew, he had
any intention to block investigation of the tragedy. Ismay
asserted that he did not know there was to be an investigation
until the Cunarder docked.

Mr. William E. Carter, of Bryn Mawr, who, with his family, was
saved, confirmed Mr. Ismay's assertions.

"Mr. Ismay's statement is absolutely correct," said Mr. Carter.
"There were no women on the deck when that boat was launched.
We were the very last to leave the deck, and we entered the life-
boat because there were no women to enter it.

"The deck was deserted when the boat was launched, and Mr.
Ismay and myself decided that we might as well enter the boat
and pull away from the wreck. If he wants me, I assume that he
will write to me.

"I can say nothing, however, that he has not already said, as
our narratives are identical; the circumstances under which we
were rescued from the Titanic were similar. We left the boat
together and were picked up together, and, further than that,
we were the very last to leave the deck.

"I am ready to go to Washington to testify to the truth of Mr.
Ismay's statement, and also to give my own account at any time
I may be called upon. If Mr. Ismay writes to me, asking that I
give a detailed account of our rescue, I will do so.

CHAPTER XXIII

The Financial Loss

TITANIC NOT FULLY INSURED—VALUABLE CARGO AND MAIL—
NO CHANCE FOR SALVAGE—LIFE INSURANCE LOSS—LOSS TO THE
CARPATHIA.

S O GREAT was the interest in the tragedy and so profound
the grief at the tremendous loss of life that for a time the
financial loss was not considered. It was, however, the
biggest ever suffered by marine insurance brokers.

The value of the policy covering the vessel against all ordinary risks was $5,000,000, but the whole of this amount was
not insured, because British and Continental markets were not
big enough to swallow it. The actual amount of insurance was
$3,700,000, of which the owners themselves held $750,000.

As to the cargo, it was insured by the shippers. The company
has nothing to do with the insurance of the cargo, which, according to the company's manifest, was conservatively estimated at
about $420,000. Cargo, however, was a secondary matter, so far
as the Titanic was concerned. The ship was built for high-priced
passengers, and what little cargo she carried was also of the kind
that demanded quick transportation. The Titanic's freight was
for the most part what is known as high-class package freight,
consisting of such articles as fine laces, ostrich feathers, wines,
liquors and fancy food commodities.

LOST MAIL MAY COST MILLIONS

Prior to the sailing of the vessel the postal authorities of Southampton cabled the New York authorities that 3435 bags of mail matter were on board.

"In a load of 3500 bags," said Postmaster Morgan, of New York, "it is a safe estimate to say that 200 contained registered mail. The size of registered mail packages varies greatly, but 1000 packages for each mail bag should be a conservative guess. That would mean that 200,000 registered packages and letters went down with the Titanic.

"This does not mean, however, that Great Britain will be held financially responsible for all these losses. There were probably thousands of registered packages from the Continent, and in such cases the countries of origin will have to reimburse the senders. Moreover, in the case of money being sent in great quantities, it is usual to insure the registry over and above the limit of responsibility set by the country of origin.

"Probably if there were any shipping of securities mounting up to thousands of dollars, it will be the insurance companies which will bear the loss, and not the European post offices at all."

In the case of money orders, the postmaster explained, there would be no loss, except of time, as duplicates promptly would be shipped without further expense.

The postmaster did not know the exact sum which the various European countries set as the limit of their guarantee in registered mail. In America it is $50.

Underwriters will probably have to meet heavy claims of passengers for luggage, including jewelry. Pearls of one American woman insured in London were valued at $240,000.

NO CHANCE FOR SALVAGE

The Titanic and her valuable cargo can never be recovered, said the White Star Line officials.

"Sinking in mid-ocean, at the depth which prevails where the accident occurred," said Captain James Parton, manager of the company, "absolutely precludes any hopes of salvage."

LIFE INSURANCE LOSS

In the life insurance offices there was much figuring over the lists of those thought to be lost aboard the Titanic. Nothing but rough estimates of the company's losses through the wreck were given out.

LOSS TO THE CARPATHIA

The loss to the Carpathia, too, was considerable. It is, of course, the habit of all good steamship lines to go out of their way and cheerfully submit to financial loss when it comes to succoring the distressed or the imperiled at sea. Therefore, the Cunard Line in extending the courtesies of the sea to the survivors of the Titanic asked for nothing more than the mere acknowledgment of the little act of kindness. The return of the Carpathia cost the line close to $10,000.

She was delayed on her way to the Mediterranean at least ten days and was obliged to coal and provision again, as the extra 800 odd passengers she was carrying reduced her large allowance for her long voyage to the Mediterranean and the Adriatic very much.

CHAPTER XXIV

OPINIONS OF EXPERTS

CAPTAIN E. K. RODEN, LEWIS NIXON, GENERAL GREELY AND ROBERT H. KIRK POINT OUT LESSONS TAUGHT BY TITANIC DISASTER AND NEEDED CHANGES IN CONSTRUCTION.

THE tremendous loss of life necessarily aroused a discussion as to the cause of the disaster, and the prevailing opinion seemed to be that the present tendency in shipbuilding was to sacrifice safety to luxury.

Captain Roden, a well-known Swedish navigator, had written an article maintaining this theory in the Navy, a monthly service magazine, in November, 1910. With seeming prophetic insight he had mentioned the Titanic by name and portrayed some of the dangers to which shipbuilding for luxury was leading.

He pointed out that the new steamships, the Olympic and Titanic, would be the finest vessels afloat, no expense being spared to attain every conceivable comfort for which men or women of means could possibly ask—staterooms with private shower-baths, a swimming pool large enough for diving, a ballroom covering an entire upper deck, a gymnasium, elaborate cafés, a sun deck representing a flower garden, and other luxuries.

After forcibly pointing out the provisions that should be made for the protection of life, Captain Roden wrote in conclusion:

"If the men controlling passenger ships, from the ocean liner down to the excursion barge, were equally disposed to equip their vessels with the best safety appliances as they are to devise and adopt implements of comfort and luxury, the advantage to themselves as well as to their patrons would be plainly apparent."

VIEW OF LEWIS NIXON

Lewis Nixon, the eminent naval architect and designer of the battleship Oregon, contributed a very interesting comment. He said in part:

"Here was a vessel presumed, and I think rightly so, to be the perfection of the naval architect's art, yet sunk in a few hours by an accident common to North Atlantic navigation.

THE UNSINKABLE SHIP

"An unsinkable ship is possible, but it would be of little use except for flotation. It may be said that vessels cannot be built to withstand such an accident.

"We might very greatly subdivide the forward compartments, where much space is lost at best, making the forward end, while amply strong for navigation purposes, of such construction that it would collapse and take up some of the energy of impact; then tie this to very much stronger sections farther aft. Many such plans will be proposed by those who do not realize the momentum of a great vessel which will snap great cables like ribbons, when the motion of the vessel is not perceptible to the eye.

"The proper plan is to avoid the accident, and if an accident is unavoidable to minimize the loss of life and property."

VIEW OF ROBERT H. KIRK

The Titanic disaster was discussed by Robert H. Kirk, who installed the compartment doors in the ships of the United States Navy. Mr. Kirk's opinion follows:

"The Titanic's disaster will cause endless speculation as to how similar disasters may be avoided in the future.

BULKHEAD DOORS PROBABLY OPEN

"The Titanic had bulkheads, plenty of them, for the rules of the British Board of Trade and of Lloyds are very specific and require enough compartments to insure floating of the ship though several may be flooded. She also had doors in the bulkheads, and probably plenty of them, for she was enormous and needed easy access from one compartment to another. It will probably never be known how few of these doors were closed when she struck the iceberg, but the probability is that many were open, for in the confusion attending such a crash the crews have a multitude of duties to perform, and closing a door with water rushing through it is more of a task than human muscle and bravery can accomplish.

"A Lloyds surveyor in testing one of these hand-operated doors started two men on the main deck to close it. They worked four hours before they had carried out his order. If all the doors on the ship had worked as badly as this one, what would have happened in event of accident?"

MANIA FOR SPEED

General Adolphus W. Greely, U. S. A., noted American traveler and Arctic explorer, vehemently denounced the sinking of the Titanic and the loss of over 1600 souls as a terrible sacrifice to the American mania for speed. He gave his opinion that the Titanic came to grief through an attempt on the part of the steamship management to establish a new record by the vessel on her maiden voyage.

The Titanic, General Greely declared, had absolutely no business above Cape Race and north of Sable Island on the trip on which she went to her doom. Choosing the northern route brought about the dire disaster, in his mind, and it was the saving of three hours for the sake of a new record that ended in the collision with the tragic victory for the ghostlike monster out of the far north.

It was the opinion of General Greely, capable of judging after his many trips in quest of the pole, that neither Captain Smith nor any of his officers saw the giant iceberg which encompassed their ruin until they were right upon it. Then, the ship was plunging ahead at such frightful velocity that the Titanic was too close to avert striking the barrier lined up across its path.

CHAPTER XXV

THE SENATORIAL INVESTIGATION

PROMPT ACTION OF THE GOVERNMENT—SENATE COMMITTEE
PROBES DISASTER AND BRINGS OUT DETAILS—TESTIMONY OF
ISMAY, OFFICERS, CREW, PASSENGERS AND OTHER WITNESSES.

PUBLIC sentiment with regard to the Titanic disaster was
reflected in the prompt action of the United States
Government.

On April 17th the Senate, without a dissenting vote, ordered
an investigation of the wreck of the Titanic, with particular ref-
erence to the inadequacy of life-saving boats and apparatus.
The resolution also directed inquiry into the use by the Titanic
of the northern course "over a route commonly regarded as dangerous from icebergs."

Besides investigating the disaster, the committee was directed
to look into the feasibility of international agreements for the further protection of ocean traffic.

The Senate Committee on Commerce, in whose charge the
investigation was placed, immediately appointed the following
sub-committee to conduct the gathering of evidence and the
examination of witnesses:

Senator William Alden Smith of Michigan, chairman; Senator
Francis Newlands of Nevada, Senator Jonathan Bourne, Jr., of
Oregon, Senator George C. Perkins of California, Senator

Theodore E. Burton of Ohio, Senator Furnifold McL. Simmons of North Carolina and Senator Duncan U. Fletcher of Florida.

The Senate Committee began its investigation in New York on Friday, April 19th, the morning after the arrival of the Carpathia.

Ismay, the first witness, came to the witness chair with a smile upon his face. He was sworn and then told the committee that he made the voyage on the Titanic only as a voluntary passenger. Nobody designated him to come to see how the newly launched monster would behave on the initial trip. He said that no money was spared in the construction, and as she was built on commission there was no need for the builders to slight the work for their own benefit. The accident had happened on Sunday night, April 14th.

"I was in bed and asleep," he said. "The ship was not going at full speed, as has been printed, because full speed would be from seventy-eight to eighty revolutions, and we were making only seventy-five. After the impact with the iceberg I dressed and went on deck. I asked the steward what the matter was and he told me. Then I went to Captain Smith and asked him if the ship was in danger and he told me he thought she was. "

Ismay said that he went on the bridge and remained there for some time and then lent a hand in getting the life-boats ready. He helped to get the women and children into the boats.

Ismay said that no other executive officer of the steamship company was on board, which practically made him the sole master of the vessel the minute it passed beyond the control of the captain and his fellow-officers. But Ismay, seeming to scent the drift of the questions, said that he never interfered in any way with the handling of the ship.

Ismay was asked to give more particulars about his departure from the ship. He said:

"The boat was ready to be lowered away and the officer called out if there were any more women or children to go or any more passengers on deck, but there was none, and I got on board."

CAPTAIN ROSTRON'S TESTIMONY

Captain Rostron, of the Carpathia, followed Mr. Ismay. He said the first message received from the Titanic was that she was in immediate danger. "I gave the order to turn the ship around as soon as the Titanic had given her position. I set a course to pick up the Titanic, which was fifty-eight miles west of my position. I sent for the chief engineer, told him to put on another watch of stokers and make all speed for the Titanic. I told the first officer

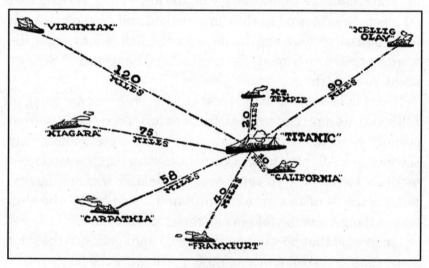

DIAGRAM SHOWING THE PROXIMITY OF OTHER STEAMSHIPS TO THE TITANIC ON NIGHT OF DISASTER.

to stop all deck work, get out the life-boats and be ready for any emergency. The chief steward and doctors of the Carpathia I called to my office and instructed as to their duties. The English doctor was assigned to the first class dining room, the Italian doctor to the second class dining room, the Hungarian doctor to the third class dining room. They were instructed to be ready with all supplies necessary for any emergency."

The Captain told in detail of the arrangements made to prepare the life-boats and the ship for the receipt of the survivors.

WEEPS AS HE TELLS STORY

Then with tears filling his eyes, Captain Rostron said he called the purser. "I told him," said Captain Rostron, "I wanted to hold a service of prayer—thanksgiving for the living and a funeral service for the dead. I went to Mr. Ismay. He told me to take full charge. An Episcopal clergyman was found among the passengers and he conducted the services.

TITANIC WAS A "LIFE-BOAT"

Captain Rostron said that the Carpathia had twenty life-boats of her own, in accordance with the British regulations.

"Wouldn't that indicate that the regulations are out of date, your ship being much smaller than the Titanic, which also carried twenty life-boats? " Senator Smith asked.

"No. The Titanic was supposed to be a life-boat herself."

WIRELESS FAILED

Why so few messages came from the Carpathia was gone into. Captain Rostron declared the first messages, all substantially the same, were sent to the White Star Line, the Cunard Line and the Associated Press. Then the first and second cabin passenger lists were sent, when the wireless failed.

Senator Smith said some complaint had been heard that the Carpathia had not answered President Taft's inquiry for Major Butt. Captain Rostron declared a reply was sent, "Not on board."

Captain Rostron declared he issued orders for no messages to be sent except upon orders from him, and for official business to go first, then private messages from the Titanic survivors in order of filing.

Absolutely no censorship was exercised, he said. The wireless continued working all the way in, the Marconi operator being constantly at the key.

Guglielmo Marconi, the wireless inventor, was the next witness.

Marconi said he was chairman of the British Marconi Company. Under instructions of the company, he said, operators must take their orders from the captain of the ship on which they are employed.

"Do the regulations prescribe whether one or two operators should be aboard the ocean vessels?"

"Yes, on ships like the late Titanic and Olympic two are carried," said Marconi. "The Carpathia, a smaller boat, carries one. The Carpathia's wireless apparatus is a short-distance equipment."

TITANIC WELL EQUIPPED

"Do you consider that the Titanic was equipped with the latest improved wireless apparatus?"

"Yes; I should say that it had the very best."

"Did you hear the captain of the Carpathia say, in his testimony, that they caught this distress message from the Titanic almost providentially?" asked Senator Smith.

"Yes, I did. It was absolutely providential."

"Is there any signal for the operator if he is not at his post?"

"I think there is none," said Marconi.

"Ought it not to be incumbent upon ships to have an operator always at the key?"

"Yes; but shipowners don't like to carry two operators when they can get along with one. The smaller boat owners do not like the expense of two operators."

SECOND OFFICER TESTIFIED

Charles Herbert Lightoller, second officer of the Titanic, followed Marconi on the stand. Mr. Lightoller said he understood the maximum speed of the Titanic, as shown by its trial tests, to have been twenty-two and a half to twenty three knots. Senator Smith asked if the rule requiring life-saving apparatus to be in each room for each passenger was complied with.

"Everything was complete," said Lightoller. "Sixteen life-boats, of which four were collapsible, were on the Titanic," he added. During the tests, he said, Captain Clark, of the British Board of Trade, was aboard the Titanic to inspect its life-saving equipment.

"How thorough are these captains of the Board of Trade in inspecting ships?" asked Senator Smith.

"Captain Clark is so thorough that we called him a nuisance."

TITANIC FILLED RAPIDLY

After testifying to the circumstances under which the life boats were filled and lowered, Lightoller continued. "The boat's deck was only ten feet from the water when I lowered the sixth boat. When we lowered the first, the distance to the water was seventy feet."

"If the same course was pursued on the starboard side as you pursued on the port, in filling boats, how do you account for so many members of the crew being saved?" asked Chairman Smith.

"I have inquired especially and have found that for every six persons picked up, five were either firemen or stewards."

COTTAM TELLS HIS STORY

Thomas, of Liverpool, the Marconi operator on the Carpathia, was the next witness. Cottam said that he was about ready to retire Sunday night, having partially removed his clothes, and was waiting for a reply to a message to the Parisian when he heard Cape Cod trying to call the Titanic. Cottam called the Titanic operator to inform him of the fact, and received the reply. 'Come at once; this is a distress message. C. Q. D.'

"What did you do then?"

"I confirmed the distress message by asking the Titanic if I should report the distress message to the captain of the Carpathia."

"How much time elapsed after you received the Titanic's distress message before you reported it to Captain Rostron?"

"About a couple of minutes," Cottam answered.

COTTAM RECALLED

When the committee resumed the investigation on April 20th, Cottam was recalled to the stand.

Senator Smith asked the witness if he had received any messages from the time the Carpathia left the scene of the disaster until it reached New York. The purpose of this question was to discover whether any official had sought to keep back the news of the disaster.

"No, sir," answered Cottam. "I reported the entire matter myself to the steamship Baltic at 10.30 o'clock Monday morning. I told her we had been to the wreck and had picked up as many of the passengers as we could."

Cottam denied that he had sent any message that all passengers had been saved, or anything on which such a report could be based.

Cottam said he was at work Monday and until Wednesday. He repeated his testimony of the previous day and said he had been without sleep throughout Sunday, Monday, Tuesday and until late Wednesday afternoon when he had been relieved by Bride.

"Did you or Bride send any message declaring that the Titanic was being towed into Halifax?"

"No, sir," said the witness, with emphasis.

MARCONI EXPLAINS

In an effort to determine whether the signal "C. Q. D." might not have been misunderstood by passing ships, Senator Smith called upon Mr. Marconi.

"The 'C. Q.,'" said Marconi, "is an international signal which meant that all stations should cease sending except the one using the call. The 'D.' was added to indicate danger. The call, however, now has been superseded by the universal call, 'S. O. S.'"

BRIDE ON THE STAND

Harold S. Bride, the sole surviving operator of the Titanic, was then called.

Bride said he knew the Frankfurt was nearer than the Carpathia when he called for assistance, but that he ceased his efforts to communicate with the former because her operator persisted in asking, "What is the matter?" despite Bride's message that the ship was in distress.

Time after time Senator Smith asked in many varying forms why the Titanic did not explain its condition to the Frankfurt.

"Any operator receiving 'C. Q. D.' and the position of the ship, if he is on the job," said Bride, "would tell the captain at once."

Marconi again testified to the distress signals and said that the Frankfurt was equipped with Marconi wireless. He said that the receipt of the signal "C. Q. D." by the Frankfurt's operator should have been all-sufficient to send the Frankfurt to the immediate rescue.

ALL APPEALS RECEIVED

Under questioning by Senator Smith, Bride said that undoubtedly the Frankfurt received all of the urgent appeals for help sent subsequently to the Carpathia.

INVESTIGATION CARRIED TO WASHINGTON

The first witness when the investigation was resumed in Washington on April 22d was P. A. S. Franklin, vice-president of the International Mercantile Marine Company.

Franklin testified that he had had no communication with Captain Smith during the Titanic's voyage, nor with Ismay, except one cable from Southampton.

Senator Smith then showed Mr. Franklin the telegram received by Congressman Hughes, of West Virginia, from the White Star Line, dated New York, April 15th, and addressed to J. A. Hughes, Huntington, W Va., as follows:

"Titanic proceeding to Halifax. Passengers probably land on Wednesday. All safe.

(Signed) — "THE WHITE STAR LINE. "

TELEGRAM A MYSTERY

"I ask you," continued the senator, "whether you know about the sending of that telegram, by whom it was authorized and from whom it was sent?"

"I do not, sir," said Franklin. "since it was mentioned at the Waldorf Saturday we have had the entire passenger staff examined and we cannot find out."

Asked when he first knew that the Titanic had sunk, Franklin said he first knew it about 6.27 P. M., Monday.

Mr. Franklin then produced a thick package of telegrams which he had received in relation to the disaster.

"About twenty minutes of two on Monday morning," said he, "I was awakened by a telephone bell, and was called by a reporter for some paper who informed me that the Titanic had met with an accident and was sinking. I asked him where he got the information. He told me that it had come by wireless from the steamship Virginian, which had been appealed to by the Titanic for aid."

Mr. Franklin said he called up the White Star docks, but they had no information, and he then appealed to the Associated Press, and there was read to him a dispatch from Cape Race advising him of the accident.

"I asked the Associated Press," said Mr. Franklin, "not to send out the dispatch until we had more detailed information, in order to avoid causing unnecessary alarm. I was told, however, that the story already had been sent."

The reassuring statements sent out by the line in the early hours of the disaster next were made the subject of inquiry

"Tell the committee on what you based those statements," directed Senator Smith.

"We based them on reports and rumors received at Cape Race by individuals and by the newspapers. They were rumors, and we could not place our finger on anything authentic."

FIRST DEFINITE NEWS

"At 6.20 or 6.30 Monday evening," Mr. Franklin continued, "a message was received telling the fateful news that the Carpathia reached the Titanic and found nothing but boats and wreckage; that the Titanic had foundered at 2.20 a.m. in 41.16 north, 50.14 west; that the Carpathia picked up all the boats and had on board about 675 Titanic survivors—passengers and crew.

"It was such a terrible shock that it took me several moments to think what to do. Then I went downstairs to the reporters, I began to read the message, holding it high in my hand. I had read only to the second line, which said that the Titanic had sunk, when there was not a reporter left—they were so anxious to get to the telephones.

SAFETY EQUIPMENT

"The Titanic's equipment was in excess of the law," said the witness. "It carried its clearance in the shape of a certificate from the British Board of Trade. I might say that no vessel can leave a British port without a certificate that it is equipped to care for human lives aboard in case of accident. It is the law."

"Do you know of anyone, any officer or man or any official, whom you deem could be held responsible for the accident and its attendant loss of life?"

"Positively not. No one thought such an accident could happen. It was undreamed of. I think it would be absurd to try to hold some individual responsible. Every precaution was taken; that the precautions were of no avail is a source of the deepest sorrow. But the accident was unavoidable."

FOURTH OFFICER TESTIFIES

J. B. Boxhall, the fourth officer, was then questioned.

"Were there any drills or any inspection before the Titanic sailed?" he was asked.

"Both," said the witness. "The men were mustered and the life-boats lowered in the presence of the inspectors from the Board of Trade."

"How many boats were lowered?"

"Jut two, sir."

"One on each side of the ship?"

"No, sir. They were both on the same side. We were lying in dock."

The witness said he did not know whether the lowering tackle ran free or not on that occasion.

"In lowering the life-boats at the test, did the gear work satisfactorily?"

"So far as I know. "

In lowering a life-boat, he said, first the boat has to be cleared, chocks knocked down and the boat hangs free. Then the davits are screwed out to the ship's side and the boat lowered.

At the time of the tests all officers of the Titanic were present.

Boxhall said that under the weather conditions experienced at the time of the collision the life-boats were supposed to carry sixty-five persons. Under the regulations of the British Board of Trade, in addition to the oars, there were in the boats water breakers, water dippers, bread, bailers, mast and sail and lights and a supply of oil. All of these supplies, said Boxhall, were in the boats when the Titanic left Belfast. He could not say whether they were in when the vessel left Southampton.

"Now," repeated Senator Smith, "suppose the weather was clear and the sky unruffled, as it was at the time of the disaster, how many would the boat hold?"

"Really, I don't know. It would depend largely upon the people who were to enter. If they did as they were told I believe each boat could accommodate sixty-five persons."

Boxhall testified to the sobriety and good habits of his superior and brother officers.

NO TRACE OF DAMAGE INSIDE

Boxhall said he went down to the steerage, inspected all the decks in the vicinity of where the ship had struck, found no traces of any damage and went directly to the bridge and so reported.

CARPENTER FOUND LEAKS

"The captain ordered me to send a carpenter to sound the ship, but I found a carpenter coming up with the announcement that the ship was taking water. In the mail room I found mail sacks floating about while the clerks were at work. I went to the bridge and reported, and the captain ordered the life-boats to be made ready."

Boxhall testified that at Captain Smith's orders he took word of the ship's position to the wireless operators.

"What position was that?

"Forty-one forty-six north, fifty fourteen west."

"Was that the last position taken?"

After that Boxhall went back to the life-boats, where there were many men and women. He said they had been provided with life-belts.

DISTRESS ROCKETS FIRED

"After that I was on the bridge most of the time sending out distress signals, trying to attract the attention of boats ahead," he said. "I sent up distress rockets until I left the ship, to try to attract the attention of a ship directly ahead. I had seen her lights. She seemed to be meeting us and was not far away. She got close enough, so she seemed to me, to read our Morse electric signals."

"Suppose you had a powerful search light on the Titanic, could you not have thrown a beam on the vessel and have compelled her attention?"

"We might."

H. J. Pitman, the third officer of the ship, was the first witness on April 23d. By a series of searching questions Senator Fletcher brought out the fact that when the collision occurred the titanic was going at the greatest speed attained during the trip, even though the ship was entering the Grand Banks and had been advised on the presence of ice.

Frederick Fleet, a sailor and lookout man on Titanic, followed Pitman on the stand. Fleet said he had had five or six years' experience at sea and was lookout on the Oceanic prior to going on the Titanic. He was in the crow's nest at the time of the collision.

Fleet stated that he had kept a sharp lookout for ice, and testified to seeing the iceberg and signaling the bridge.

Fleet acknowledged that if he had been aided in his observations by a good glass he probably could have spied the berg into which the ship crashed in time to have warned the bridge to avoid it. Major Arthur Peuchen, of Toronto, a passenger who followed Fleet on the stand, also testified to the much greater sweep of vision afforded by binoculars and, as a yachtsman, said he believed the presence of the iceberg might have been detected in time to escape the collision had the lookout men been so equipped.

HAD ASKED FOR BINOCULARS

It was made to appear that the blame for being without glasses did not rest with the lookout men. Fleet said they had asked for them at Southampton and were told there were none for then. One glass, in a pinch, would have served in the crow's nest.

The testimony before the committee on April 24th showed that the big steamship was on the verge of a field of ice twenty or thirty miles long, if she had not actually entered it, when the accident occurred.

The committee tried to discover whether it would add to human safety if the ships were fitted with search lights so that at night objects could be seen at a greater distance. The testimony so far along this line had been conflicting. Some of the witnesses thought it would be no harm to try it, but they were all skeptical as to its value, as an iceberg would not be especially distinguishable because its bulk is mostly below the surface.

One of the witnesses said that much dependence is not placed upon the lookout, and that those lookouts who used binoculars constantly found them detrimental.

Harold G. Lowe, fifth officer of the Titanic, told the committee his part in the struggle of the survivors for life following the catastrophe. The details of this struggle have already been told in a previous chapter.

AUTHORIZED TO SELL STORY

In great detail Guglielmo Marconi, on April 25th, explained the operations of his system and told how he had authorized Operator Bride of the Titanic, and Operator Cottam, of the Carpathia, to sell their stories of the disaster after they came ashore.

In allowing the operators to sell their stories, said Mr. Marconi, there was no question of suppressing or monopolizing the news. He had done everything he could, he said, to have the country informed as quickly as possible of the details of the disaster. That was why he was particularly glad for the narratives of such important witnesses as the operators to receive publication, regardless of the papers that published them.

He repeated the testimony of Cottam that every effort had been made to get legitimate dispatches ashore. The cruiser Chester, he said, had been answered as fully as possible, though it was not known at the time that its queries came from the President of the United States. The Salem, he said, had never got in touch with the Carpathia operator.

Senator Newlands suggested that the telegrams, some signed by the name of Mr. Sammis and some with the name of Marconi, directing Cottam to "keep his mouth shut" and hold out for figures on his story, was sent only as the Carpathia was entering New York harbor, when there was no longer need for sending official or private messages from the rescuing ship. There had been an impression before, he said, that the messages had been sent to Cottam when the ship was far at sea, when they might have meant that he was to hold back messages relieving the anxiety of those on shore.

SAW DISTRESS ROCKETS

Ernest Gill, a donkey engineman on the steamship Californian, was the first witness on April 26th. He said that Captain Stanley Lord, of the Californian, refused later to go to the aid of the Titanic, the rockets from which could be plainly seen. He says the captain was apprised of these signals, but made no effort to get up steam and go to the rescue. The Californian was drifting with the floe. So indignant did he become, said Gill, that he endeavored to recruit a committee of protest from among the crew, but the men failed him.

Captain Lord entered a sweeping denial of Gill's accusations and read from the Californian's log to support his contention. Cyril Evans, the Californian's wireless operator, however, told of hearing much talk among the crew, who were critical of the captain's course. Gill, he said, told him he expected to get $500 for his story when the ship reached Boston.

Evans told of having warned the Titanic only a brief time before the great vessel crashed into the berg that the sea was crowded with ice. The Titanic's operators, he said, at the time were working with the wireless station at Cape Race, and they told him to "shut up" and keep out. Within a half hour the pride of the sea was crumpled and sinking.

Members of the committee who examined individually the British sailors and stewards of the Titanic's crew prepared a report of their investigations for the full committee. This testimony was ordered to be incorporated in the record of the hearings.

Most of this testimony was but a repetition of experiences similar to the many already related by those who got away in the life boats.

On April 27th, Captain James H. Moore, of the steamship Mount Temple, who hurried to the Titanic in response to wireless calls for help, told of the great stretch of field ice which held him off. Within his view from the bridge he discerned, he said, a strange steamship, probably a "tramp," and a schooner which was making her way out of the ice. The lights of this schooner, he thought, probably were those seen by the anxious survivors of the Titanic and which they were frantically trying to reach.

WOMEN AT HEARING WEEP

Steward Crawford also related a thrilling story in regard to loading the life-boats with women first. He told of several instances that came under his observation of women throwing their arms around their husbands and crying out that they would not leave the ship without them. The pathetic recital caused several women at the hearing to weep, and all within earshot of the steward's story were thrilled.

ANDREWS WAS BRAVE

Stories that Mr. Andrews, the designer of the ship, had tried to disguise the extent of danger were absolutely denied by Henry Samuel Etches, his bedroom steward, who told the committee how Mr. Andrews urged women back to their cabins to dress more warmly and to put on life-belts.

The steward, whose duty it was to serve Major Butt and his party, told how he did not see the Major at dinner the evening of the disaster as he was dining with a private party in the restaurant. William Burke, a first class steward, told of serving dinner at 7.15 o'clock to Mr. and Mrs. Straus, and later Mrs. Straus' refusal to leave her husband was again told to the committee. A bedroom steward told of a quiet conversation with Benjamin Guggenheim, Senator Guggenheim's brother, after the accident and shortly before the Titanic settled in the plunge that was to be his death.

On April 29th Marconi produced copies of several messages which passed between the Marconi office and the Carpathia in an effort to get definite information of the wreck and the survivors.

Marconi and F. M. Sammis, chief engineer of the American

Marconi Company, both acknowledged that a mistake had been made in sending messages to Bride and Cottam on board the Carpathia not to give out any news until they had seen Marconi and Sammis.

The senatorial committee investigating the Titanic disaster has served several good purposes. It has, officially established the fact that all nations are censurable for insufficient, antiquated safety regulations on ocean vessels, and it has emphasized the imperative necessity for united action among all maritime countries to revise these laws and adapt them to changed conditions.

The committee reported its findings as, follows:

GENERAL CONCLUSIONS

No particular person was named as being responsible, though attention was called to the fact that on the day of the disaster three distinct warnings of ice were sent to Captain Smith. J. Bruce Ismay, managing director of the White Star Line, was not held responsible for the ship's high speed. In fact, he was barely mentioned in the report.

Ice positions, so definitely reported to the Titanic just preceding the accident, located ice on both sides of the lane in which she was traveling. No discussion took place among the officers, no conference was called to consider these warnings, no heed was given to them. The speed was not relaxed, the lookout was not increased.

The supposedly water-tight compartments of the Titanic were not water-tight, because of the non-water-tight condition of the decks where the transverse bulkheads ended.

The steamship Californian, controlled by the same concern as the Titanic, was nearer the sinking steamship than the nineteen miles reported by her captain, and her officers and crew saw the distress signals of the Titanic and failed to respond to them in accordance with the dictates of humanity international usage and the requirements of law. Had assistance been promptly proffered the Californian might have had the profound distinction of the lives of the passengers and crew of the Titanic.

The mysterious lights on an unknown ship, seen by the passengers on the Titanic, undoubtedly were on the Californian, less than nineteen miles away.

Eight ships, all equipped with wireless, were in the vicinity of the Titanic, the Olympic farthest away—512 miles.

The full capacity of the Titanic's life-boats was not utilized, because, while only 705 persons were saved, the ship's boats could have carried 1176.

No general alarm was sounded, no whistle blown and no systematic warning was given to the endangered passengers, and it was fifteen or twenty minutes after the collision before Captain Smith ordered the Titanic's wireless operator to send out a distress message.

The Titanic's crew were only meagerly acquainted with their positions and duties in an accident and only one drill was held before the maiden trip. Many of the crew joined the ship only a few hours before she sailed and were in ignorance of their positions until the following Friday.

Many more lives could have been saved had the survivors been concentrated in a few life-boats, and had the boats thus released returned to the wreck for others.

The first official information of the disaster was the message from Captain Haddock, of the Olympic, received by the White Star Line at 6.16 P. M., Monday, April 15. In the face of this information a message reporting the Titanic being towed to Halifax was sent to Representative J. A. Hughes, at Huntington, W. Va., at 7.51 P. M. that day. The message was delivered to the Western Union office in the same building as the White Star Line offices.

"Whoever sent this message," says the report," under the circumstances, is guilty of the most reprehensible conduct."

The wireless operator on the Carpathia was not duly vigilant in handling his messages after the accident.

The practice of allowing wireless operators to sell their stories should be stopped.

RECOMMENDATIONS

It was recommended that all ships carrying more than 100 passengers should have two searchlights.

That a revision be made of steamship inspection laws of foreign countries to conform to the standard proposed in the United States.

That every ship be required to carry sufficient life-boats for all passengers and crew.

That the use of wireless be regulated to prevent interference by amateurs, and that all ships have a wireless operator on constant duty.

Detailed recommendations were made as to water-tight bulkhead construction on ocean-going ships. Bulkheads should be so spaced that any two adjacent compartments of a ship might be flooded without sinking.

Transverse bulkheads forward and abaft the machinery should be continued watertight to the uppermost continuous structural deck, and this deck should be fitted water-tight.